imperfectly
PERFECT

A Devotional for the *Transformed* Everyday Sinner

Nice meeting you Lisa ♡ In Christ's love, Laura

Laura E. Sandretti

Imperfectly Perfect: A Devotional for the Transformed, Everyday Sinner
Copyrighted © 2019 by Laura E. Sandretti
ISBN 978-1-64538-088-7
First Edition

Imperfectly Perfect: A Devotional for the Transformed, Everyday Sinner
by Laura E. Sandretti

For information, please contact:

Orange Hat Publishing
www.orangehatpublishing.com
Waukesha, WI

Cover photo © Photography by Jill Ann
Cover and interior design by Kaeley Dunteman
Edited by Lauren Blue

For Chris.

For reading my blog posts, even when you were tired.

For encouraging all my endeavors, even though it means more work, time alone, and chaos for you.

For always loving me and giving me grace, the hot (though in Christ, perfect) mess I am.

I love you...

Always,
Laura

Table of Contents

Introduction *8*

Week 1: My Autoimmune Dis-ease *12*

Week 2: Struggling with ADD *16*

Week 3: The Slow Work of God *20*

Week 4: I Don't Know *24*

Week 5: Tired *28*

Week 6: My Problem with Memorizing Scripture *32*

Week 7: A Closet Evangelical *36*

Week 8: Does Church Work? *40*

Week 9: Here's Your Sign *44*

Week 10: God's On My Side? *50*

Week 11: I Am the Church *54*

Week 12: Driving Slowly, in Jesus' Name *58*

Week 13: Why I Like Arguing with My Husband *62*

Week 14: Burning My AARP Card *66*

Week 15: Social Media Sabbatical *70*

Week 16: Why the Bible is Confusing *74*

Week 17: When Faith Works *78*

Week 18: When the Church Fails. Again. *82*

Week 19: Spirit-Inspired Whispers *86*

Week 20: My Murderous Rage *92*

Week 21: How to Love in the Controversial *98*

Week 22: Intolerance of Doughheads *102*

Week 23: I Can't Tell Them That *106*

Week 24: Losing My [Thick] Head *110*

Week 25: Scary Prayers *114*

Week 26: Disliking Your Husband's Wife *118*

Week 27: Where's God? *122*

Week 28: Swamp Flowers *126*

Week 29: Back to Normal *130*

Week 30: Reaching the End of My Rope *134*

Week 31: Bone Scans and Biopsies *138*

Week 32: How to Love People Who Are Hard to Like *142*

Week 33: You Prayed Once? *146*

Week 34: Why Peter's My Favorite *150*

Week 35: Who Am I, Really? *154*

Week 36: Dear Four-Years-Ago Self *158*

Week 37: Road Rage On My Way to Church *162*

Week 38: Struggling to Love *166*

Week 39: How to Love Difficult People *170*

Week 40: Lessons Along the Wait *174*

Week 41: A Death in the Family *178*

Week 42: The Tone of God's Voice *182*

Week 43: This, Again? *186*

Week 44: When Your Friend Gets Robbed *190*

Week 45: Finally Free *194*

Week 46: International Sledding Lessons *198*

Week 47: Why I Had to Stop Crying *202*

Week 48: Four Words That Are Saving My Marriage *206*

Week 49: "Help" *210*

Week 50: The [New] Voices in My Head *214*

Week 51: Fear of Snow *218*

Week 52: Jesus and Me at the Airport *222*

About the Author *226*

Introduction

I came to faith in Jesus Christ in my late twenties because I was a mess.

I struggled with many things, including, but not limited to, fear and anxiety, low self-esteem, and anger issues. Before my first child was born, I began attending a church that was different from any other church I had ever attended. There, I learned what it meant to have a relationship with Jesus Christ and how the Bible relates to our lives. I used to associate churches with rules, judgmental people, and a lot of hypocrisy, but at this church, I slowly started seeing a positive correlation in my messy life the more I prayed, read, and learned about the Bible and stepped out of my comfort zone into Christian community.

Over the years, however, I guess I peaked. Instead of continuing to realize the victories and transformation I experienced as a new Christian, I felt increasingly disappointed with feeling like an everyday sinner. The more I memorized Scripture, read my Bible, and participated in Bible studies, it seemed the more disgruntled I became with my inability to look like Jesus and be the mother, wife, and woman I wanted to be. Eventually, after about fifteen years of being a disappointment to myself, I almost walked away from Christ altogether.

I began to wonder if Jesus worked and was who He said

He was. I began to question if He was loving and if I could continue following Him. But it was in that crisis of faith, which lasted about five years, that my cerebral understanding of the cross finally seeped into and saturated my heart. I began to understand grace, not on paper or for someone else, but in the depth and crevices of my soul.

I began to genuinely know, accept, and live out of the freedom and forgiveness Christ's death on the cross afforded me.

This devotional is a collection of blog posts I've written since discovering and experiencing that life-changing grace in my mess. These are everyday stories, examples, and lessons I've learned living out of the theological tension of being imperfectly perfect. Imperfect in earthly execution, but perfect in the eyes of God because of Jesus Christ.

Author and theologian Millard J. Erickson said, "The standard to be aimed for [as a believer in Christ] is complete freedom from sin. The commands to strive by the grace of God to attain that goal are too numerous to ignore." However, Erickson also explains the dichotomy of being imperfectly perfect. "It is quite possible...to be "perfect" without being entirely free from sin. That is, we can possess the fullness of Jesus Christ (Ephesians 4:13) and the full fruit of the Spirit (Galatians 5:22-23) without possessing them completely."[1]

Despite what I fail to understand about God, the Bible, and how faith manifests itself in everyday life, God has allowed me to more fully know and believe that while I function imperfectly in this life, I am perfect in God's eyes because of Christ's death for my imperfections. It is in beginning to understand this oxymoron, that I have found freedom, gratitude, and peace like

---

[1] Erickson, Millard J. *Christian Theology,* 985. Grand Rapids: Baker Academics, 2006.

I have never known, and it is my prayer that this devotional helps orient you toward your imperfect perfection as well.

It is always a fear that anything I write will seem more straightforward, entertaining, or easy to understand than digging into the Word of God and searching, waiting on, and meeting Christ intimately and personally. While what any human author writes may seem more straightforward, entertaining, and easy to understand than the Bible, it will also most certainly always be less meaningful, rich, Spirit-filled, and sufficient in meeting people where they need freedom, forgiveness, and supernatural wisdom and insight.

One of my favorite go-to books when I need counsel, insight, and challenge is a collection of 16th and 17th century Puritan prayers called *The Valley of Vision*. The preface to the book wisely warns its readers:

"This book is not intended to be read as a prayer manual. The soul learns to pray by praying, for prayer is communion with a transcendent and immanent God who on the ground of his nature and attributes calls forth all the powers of the redeemed soul in acts of total adoration and dedication."[2]

Imperfectly Perfect lacks the depth, insight, passion, contrition, and wisdom expressed by the Puritans, however, my hope for this little devotional parallels theirs. This book is not intended to be a substitute for or to take priority over daily personal prayer or time in God's living, active, and life-changing Word. My prayer is that this book will point you toward those disciplines and make you hunger for greater intimacy with God through them. Out of that greater intimacy it is also my prayer, dear sister, that you will realize and live out

---

[2] Bennett, Arthur, ed. *The Valley of Vision: A Collection of Puritan Prayers & Devotions*, xi. Carlisle, PA: The Banner of Truth Trust, 1975.

of the depth of God's perfect and passionate love for you in the thick of your everyday, imperfect messes.

•••

My Autoimmune Dis-ease

"Give us this day our daily bread."

Matthew 6:11 (NASB)

Week One

Ten years ago, I was diagnosed with an autoimmune disease that, by God's grace, has not progressed or been symptomatic, nor could I get a second opinion confirming that I had it. Recently, however, my bloodwork is indicating a progression that, in whatever form, my body is fighting against itself. Just as I did ten years ago, I'm opting first to try and stave off illness by eating a plant-based diet.

I was dreading the thought of becoming a gluten-free vegan. The last time I ate like this after my first diagnosis, I felt deprived and unsatisfied. It's difficult to eat like a rabbit, particularly when the other rabbits you live with get to eat donuts and bacon. I decided to start my herbivorous lifestyle on January 1st, but in the weeks leading up to the new year and eating habits,

I was angsty.

A few weeks ago, I spoke at a retreat with worship leader and recording artist Gretchen Jester. She sang a song she'd written about God's grace. It was inspired by a friend who loved her husband and always worried about how she'd ever survive if anything happened to him. After her husband passed away, however, this friend realized that losing him wasn't nearly as torturous and painful as all the years she had spent worrying about losing him, because God's grace, as Gretchen reminded us, isn't for the hypothetical:

"There is no grace, for what hasn't happened yet. So, I will let go of fear of future things.

There is no peace for what hasn't happened yet. So, I will rest in you when I cannot see.

So, I will hold onto hope for future things. He gives me grace, for only this moment."

Whether it's eating kale, sending my kids to college, or getting older, Gretchen's song is true. Anxiety is, on many levels, worse than actuality. It's what Corrie ten Boom's father told her in the midst of persecution from the Nazis:

"Tell me," her father wisely responded, "when you take a train trip from Haarlem to Amsterdam, when do I give you the money for the ticket? Three weeks before?"

"No, Daddy, you give me the money for the ticket just before we get on the train."

"That is right," he replied, "and so it is with God's strength. Our wise Father in heaven knows when you are going to need things too. Today you do not need the strength to be a martyr. But as soon as you are called upon for the honor of facing death for Jesus, He will supply the strength you need—just in time."[3]

What are you worrying about that hasn't happened yet (and, in reality, may never happen)? Except for fried cheese curds, I don't miss most of what I used to eat. By God's grace, I'm adjusting well (most days) to my nest emptying. Instead of dreading what hasn't happened yet, I'm trying to hold onto hope for future things. I'm trying to trust God will provide immeasurably more...

Just in time.

• • • •

    [3] ten Boom, Corrie. *The Hiding Place*, 44. Grand Rapids: Bantam Books, 1984.

To Think About

What are you worrying about that is hypothetical?
What is causing you stress that is a future "what-if?"

This week, pray and ask God to help you find His peace that surpasses understanding. Ask Him to also help you trust that if what you're worried about does come to pass, He will sustain you with His love, presence, and strength. Ask Him to help you today to stop worrying about what may or may not happen tomorrow. And don't forget to thank Him for His amazing grace that sustains us today and gives us hope for tomorrow.

Struggling
with ADD

"Devote yourselves to prayer, being watchful and thankful."

Colossians 4:2

Week Two

Recently, I asked my friends on social media to pray for my friend's 93-year-old aunt Frances. She was just diagnosed with cancer, and her house is currently underwater thanks to a recent hurricane. I prayed for her too, but if I'm honest, I spent more time writing the social media post than I did actually praying.

I don't actually pray, a lot.

My son Casey has been battling shin splints for a year. I've prayed for him a few times, but I've spent much more time researching remedies and worrying. I've been praying for a few friends who have kids leaving for college too. Inevitably though, my mind wanders and I start thinking about dinner, bills, or important things like my new hairdo.

My biggest obstacle to actually praying is the hamster wheel inside my head. It's a wheel that turns quickly and constantly, and there are a variety of "hamsters" that spin it: anxiety, control issues, doubts, stress, my to-do list, and apparently, my hair.

So how do we actually pray?

We pray about praying.

When I asked God to help me actually pray and turn off the noise in my head, He answered in a variety of ways. When praying for Frances, God reminded me about a doctor I read about who was struggling to muster up hope or empathy for his elderly patients. The doctor then imagined one very sick, aging man as one of his own sons. How would he want someone to care for his child? Would he be okay with a doctor going through the motions because he decided their end was near anyway? Suddenly, God allowed me to pray for Frances as if she were one of my daughters going through cancer treatment and homelessness.

Casey's shins? I've been praying for over a year that everyone in my family would have a love for Christ that isn't neat, safe, and sterile, but that's passionate, deep, and life-changing. What if shin splints had a bigger purpose? How would I pray about shin splints then?

My friends whose kids are leaving home? Praying with more focus has revealed something else about my prayer life. Actually praying forces me to enter into other people's pain, and I don't always want to. I'm so thankful Hannah, my college freshman, is living at home this year. I can't and don't want to imagine her room being empty. Actually praying means praying with compassion, intentionality, and energy I don't always want to expend, but that is the heart of God and the point of prayer.

How do we actually pray? By asking God to turn off our hamster wheel whenever we pray. Martin Luther said, "Grant that I may not pray alone with the mouth; help me that I may pray from the depths of my heart." Actual prayer moves me into the presence of God. It involves my heart more than my mind. When God turns off the noise in my head and I actually pray, nothing, including my heart, remains the same.

• • • •

To Think About

Where does your mind wander when you pray? Someone once wisely told me to pray about the distractions that derail me when I'm praying. Odds are that whatever you are distracted by is what is weighing most heavily on your heart.

This week, when your mind wanders while you're praying, go with it. What better thing to do with what's really on our hearts and minds than ask the Lord about them?

The Slow
Work of God

"Be joyful in hope, patient in affliction, faithful in prayer."

Romans 12:12

Week Three

For an upcoming trip, after a fourteen-hour flight, myself and two of my children will land in China where our Chinese friend, his family, and an interpreter will be taking us to multiple cities over twelve days. We will travel by car, plane, and high-speed rail. We will see the Great Wall, go to a tiger park, and visit Disney World in Shanghai. It will be the trip of a lifetime, but here's the caveat:

I'm afraid of turbulence, heights, and unidentifiable meats. I don't speak Chinese, I hate flying, and my husband won't be with us. We cannot drink the water in China, and last month I read about a pilot flying in China who was almost sucked completely out of his cockpit window mid-flight. When my brother traveled to China, he saw a man get hit by a car on the freeway, and no one seemed to notice or be overly concerned. How is it I am traveling to a country with 1.3 billion people halfway around the world and I'm not only fearless, but excited?

Twenty years with Jesus.

When I speak at conferences about my victories over panic attacks and anxiety, women want to know how. How does God free them from fear? How should they pray, what verse should they memorize, and which Bible study should they take? How can they be free too? I wanted to be free from fear quickly, easily, and permanently when I started reading the Bible and learning about God too, but unfortunately, it doesn't usually work that way.

Psalm 27:14 says, "Wait for the LORD; Be strong and take heart and wait for the Lord." Praying, reading the Bible, and being in Christian community are vital to finding freedom from whatever keeps us in bondage. And although I've heard a million times that the Christian life a marathon, not a sprint, I still seem to always look for and expect a fast and effortless faith.

The process of being free from the things we hate, wish we could change, and hold us back is a long and arduous one. But the alternative is staying in the same places of bondage for a lifetime. The alternative is missing opportunities, experiences, and relationships because we are trapped by fear, anger, jealousy, and bitterness. The alternative is paralysis. Although I'm still afraid of many things, by God's grace, I'm not a helpless prisoner to them anymore.

The slow work of God is, in fact, slow, but slow is still progress. And slow is still better than stopped.

• • • •

To Think About

Is there something you have prayed and asked God to fix, remove, or answer, and nothing has (seemingly) changed? Is there something you have given up asking about or lost hope it will ever come to fruition? It takes strength and courage to wait on the Lord, but it is in the prayerful waiting that our faith grows and we begin to trust Him more.

This week, keep praying about something you have maybe given up praying for, and ask God for the strength and courage to continue asking until you see Him move.

I Don't Know

"And over all these virtues put on love, which binds them all together in perfect unity."

Colossians 3:14

Week Four

One of the things I repeatedly ask God to help me do is the whole "love one another" thing. I know I should love people and I want to love them, but honestly, if you drive slow in the fast lane, mess with my kids, or look at me wrong, as my friend Elle puts it:

I struggle with The Humans.

Recently, however, God has been answering my long-time prayer to love others, but not in the way I wanted it answered.

When #MeToo became a thing, it wasn't going to be my thing. Although I was a victim of sexual abuse as a preschooler, I can't change that fact, rarely think about it, and most of all, refuse to live or be seen as a victim. It was an unfortunate, one-time incident that I've existed quite happily avoiding.

Until now.

I'm currently in a discipleship group, and it's awful. I liken it to being the star on the show *Naked and Afraid* because that's what openly sharing my walls, struggles, and fears feels like. But while sharing recently in the group, I realized that although I've kept that awful childhood memory in a box, it's impacted me negatively. So I've been praying and reading the Bible to try and find freedom from my box. As pleasant as that's been (not), it has taught me something paramount.

We all have a box.

Your box is different from my box, is different from your husband's box, which is different from that lady's box who flipped you off on the freeway yesterday. Your box might be less egregious, a million times worse, or maybe happened last week. I suppose I realized cerebrally that everyone has struggles in life, but unearthing my box has taught me something I desperately needed to be reminded:

I don't know.

I don't know what your childhood was like, who hurt you, or walked out on you. I don't know the fears you've wrestled, pressures you faced yesterday, or the trauma you endured growing up. For Pete's sake, I don't know how my 40-some-year-old box impacts me, so how can I know anything about someone else's box? When I want to judge, criticize, or get offended, lately I hear, "I don't know," and it's softening me. Because just like you can't judge, know, or fix my box, I can't judge, know, or fix you or your box (and unfortunately, they're a package deal).

My box is teaching me that there's a lot I don't know. It's teaching me that because I don't know anyone else's hearts, hurts, or hang-ups, I shouldn't judge. It's giving me compassion for The Humans who are unkind, I don't understand, and normally want to avoid. "I don't know" fosters humility, empathy, and love. It's also teaching me that although our boxes are an unfortunate by-product of sin in the world, in God's economy, our box does not alter our identity or define or impact our status as children radically loved by God.

....

To Think About

"...Children radically loved by God." Therein lies the secret. The secret to how, when The Humans hurt, offend, or are insensitive to us, we can live out "I don't know." The reality is, when people are rude, hateful, or unkind, in the moment, I don't care what I don't know about them. In the moment, I don't give them the benefit of the doubt. In the moment, I struggle to like, let alone love, The Humans most days.

I am learning more and more that I will only be able to love others to the extent I know and experience God's love and grace for me. I know. I've tried hard to love people. However, the Christian faith is not about trying. It isn't about behavior modification. It is about daily remembering, re-realizing, and re-experiencing God's love by constantly asking Him, waiting for and seeing Him in our everyday hurts and struggles, and learning more about Him by reading, knowing, and wrestling with His Word.

This week, don't read the Bible to find out what you should or shouldn't do. Don't read Scripture to find the answer to your struggles. This week, only read passages in God's Word that talk about who God is and how much He loves you. Verses like Isaiah 43:1-7, Genesis 1, Psalm 103:8-12, Psalm 40:1-3, and Luke 15:11-24. I know you're busy, but sometime this week, look up those verses. Think about them. Pray about them. Memorize the one that brings tears to your eyes. His Word reminds us that we are children radically loved by Him, but I need to be reminded of that, every day, every hour, and sometimes, every minute.

Tired

"Come to me, all you who are weary and burdened, and I will give you rest. Take my yoke upon you and learn from me, for I am gentle and humble in heart, and you will find rest for your souls. For my yoke is easy and my burden is light."

Matthew 11:28-30

Week Five

For the past several months, I've been in a discipleship group trying to stop my constant obsession with worrying about what people think of me. It's been a lifetime problem that I can't seem to stop. Although I'm not fixed yet, I've been learning a lot about my "condition."

First, I've been learning to quit resisting who I am. I cry, love, and get hurt easily. I've always struggled with those things about myself, but I'm learning that there are good and bad things about the way we are innately wired. Wishing I was different is pointless and pathetic.

I'm also learning that I often don't believe the Bible. I can readily accept you're deeply loved and fearfully and wonderfully made, but if I really believed that about myself, I wouldn't care if you didn't like me. But I do. It isn't bad to believe the Bible on a partial, mainly cerebral level, but it is dangerous to fail to realize that and stay there. Abstract beliefs that aren't deeply rooted in our hearts (not just our minds), if left unrealized and unchanged, will lead us to a stagnant, complacent, and apathetic life and faith.

I'm also learning that Jesus didn't care what people thought of Him because He knew His mission and never deviated from it. So I've been working for a few months on what God's mission for my life is, and I'm discovering that God's mission for my life looks very different from my mission for my life. Discerning

God's mission is a slow process because I'm also realizing that I need to buy into and believe His mission at a deep, core level in order to abandon my own and pursue His.

Perhaps the most important thing I'm learning? It's almost impossible to love people and obsess over trying to please them.

I recently met a homeless man named CJ on Michigan Avenue when my family and I were visiting downtown Chicago. I put my hand on his shoulder and asked him his name. We talked about where he slept the night before ("Right here, in a box.") and what his options were when it got cold. Then I prayed for him, and we gave him a gift card so he could get some food. I thanked him for his amazing, joyful attitude, told him I'd pray for him, and gave him a hug.

Before I started attending this discipleship group, I would not have stopped and talked to CJ. I wouldn't have because I would've been too worried. Worried what my family, onlookers, and CJ would've thought about me. Worried about what I would say or do. Worried, predominantly and ironically, about myself.

When I'm preoccupied with pleasing people, I ignore them. When I focus on people-pleasing, I'm actually focusing on myself. People-pleasing is tiring, fruitless, and self-centered. Although I'm not cured, God in His love is helping me see that really pleasing people is caring about the condition of their souls today and tomorrow. It's accepting how God innately wired them without trying to change them. It's believing more deeply and trusting more fully who God is and His mission for my life, so I can in turn love people better, whether they love or loathe me.

. . . .

To Think About

Are you preoccupied with what others think of you? Do you try to look, speak, and act more intelligently and articulately than you believe you are? How about trying to act wealthier or more spiritual? Tiring work, isn't it? One of the ways the Lord has helped me begin to worry less about others has been to bring me to a place of physical, emotional, and mental exhaustion as I've tried to impress everyone and manage their perceptions of me.

This week, if you're in that beaten-down, ugly, and difficult place, try to thank God. He brings us to the end of ourselves to begin to free us. Don't give up! Realize that sometimes your exhaustion is God at work.

My Problem
with Memorizing
Scripture

"May the words of my mouth and the
meditation of my heart be pleasing in your
sight, O LORD, my Rock and my Redeemer."

Psalm 19:14

Week Six

This week, I was memorizing Psalm 141:3, "Set a guard over my mouth, Lord. Keep watch over the door of my lips," using an app designed to help people learn Bible verses.

Unfortunately, I haven't found an app to help me apply the verses.

The same day I was learning Psalm 141:3, I was audibly contriving a plan to make verbal retribution against a kid who had hurt one of my kids. I was also complaining to my children about another (rotten and horrible) teenager, and then I got mad at my husband Chris, who suggested that I shouldn't gossip in front of the kids. The nerve.

It's frustrating being a Christian because when I become aware of my constant failures, I know I should know better. It's frustrating because I would be happy at this point to just fail less. It's frustrating being a Christian because between the walls of my house and the confines of my head, and with the people who know the real me, I can't even come close to living out WWJD.

If I were an everyday, run-of-the-mill heathen or, minimally, I wasn't someone who wrote and spoke to people about Jesus, I wouldn't be such a disappointment to myself. I just wrote a magazine article about the benefits of memorizing Scripture, and the very day I'm memorizing a verse about controlling my mouth, I gossip about and plot the demise of my children's peers.

But it occurred to me that there is a bigger tragedy in life than being a repeated failure:

Never realizing you are one.

When my husband called me out, after a bit of pouting, I realized that he was right. I can't just go through the motions of memorizing Bible verses. I need to passionately and earnestly ask God to help make those verses my heart's cry and prayer. When I thought about how important it is to care for the poor in the inner city, God reminded me about the poor in spirit. Some of the children I was deeming entitled, disrespectful, and ungrateful don't know Jesus Christ's love. God reminded me that while I wallowed in my failure, He's called me to love them both.

Although I initially felt awful about what a hypocrite of a Christ-follower I am after all these years, I'm done beating myself up. It isn't sad that I'm a terrible Christian. We all are (it's why Christ died). It isn't sad that I keep messing up despite praying I won't (Paul had the same problem in Romans 7). It isn't sad that I don't even realize when I'm saying and doing what I shouldn't (David with Bathsheba).

What's sad are the days I've spent ignoring, legitimizing, and making excuses for my failures. Satan loves when we dwell on how bad we are instead of turning mistakes into growth opportunities. My friend Mary Beth once told me, "God loves us too much to leave us where we are." What's my new perspective on being a failure?

In Christ, there's no such thing.

••••

[4] Ortberg, John. *The Life You've Always Wanted*, 177. Grand Rapids: Zondervan, 2002.

To Think About

John Ortberg, in his amazing book *The Life You've Always Wanted*, says that "human beings have a remarkable capacity for self-deception."[4] When I read the account of David lusting over Bathsheba and having her husband killed, I used to shake my head and wonder, how? The older I get, however, the more I see how blind I can be to my own sinfulness.

Psalm 19 has a wonderful, easy-to-remember prayer that can help us avoid being masters at the art of self-deception: "May the words of my mouth and the meditation of my heart be pleasing in your sight, O Lord..."

This week, pray Psalm 19:14 and ask God to help you not only pray it, but be convicted, challenged, and changed by it as you go about your day.

A Closet Evangelical

"And hope does not disappoint us, because God has poured out his love into our hearts by the Holy Spirit, whom he has given us."

Romans 5:5

Week Seven

Someone I don't know well personally, but respect professionally, mentioned on social media that she wanted to learn more about the "evangelical world." Melanie said that it was foreign to her, but like many people who don't understand evangelical Christians, she is a good person who wants to promote love, unity, and peace, so she thought she'd check us out.

I immediately began praying about how to comment on her post in as few words as possible to avoid saying the wrong thing. But the more I prayed, the more afraid I became. Not just afraid because of me and my hypocrisy, judgmental heart, and unpopular viewpoints, but afraid that she would miss Christ because of all Christians.

When Jesus was asked what the greatest commandment was, his response was simple and two-pronged:

Love God. Love people.

I want to tell Mel that the first part is generally easy, but that second part? I struggle to love myself most days, let alone other humans. Sadly, I've found that loving the Christians, who should "know better than to (fill-in-the-blank)," is usually much harder than loving the unchurched. Also, what if she tries learning about Jesus solely through the imperfect, not-always-loving, limited knowledge of Christian bloggers and writers?

I'm afraid for Mel for other reasons too. I'm afraid because although Christ's love for us is perfect, unexplainable, and will take me a lifetime to even scratch the surface of knowing, experiencing, and understanding, God assures us in the Bible that in this life we will have trouble. Life is difficult and full of disappointments. I'm afraid because although nothing is better than knowing Christ's love, sometimes it's hard to see that in this messy world with messy people and "religion."

In addition to all the hurdles, hardships, and humans that might scare Mel away from Christ, I'm continuing to pray for Mel for other reasons, too.

I'm praying for Melanie because she's a mom raising kids in a scary world. I'm praying for her because, at the end of the day, there are more questions than answers, and although all Christians are imperfect, Christ is not. I'm praying for her because I have not been able to find hope or make any sense of cancer, natural disasters, and international political unrest outside of Jesus Christ. I'm praying for her because with or without Christ, violence, hatred, and other difficult realities still happen, but with Him, I have a shred of hope that the good guys will win someday. I'm praying because although my faith walk has been difficult and disappointing at times, I always end up coming back more in love with Jesus.

I'm praying for Melanie because although relationships, the church, and circumstances can disappoint, Jesus has given me peace, confidence in parenting despite this messed-up world, strength beyond myself, and, most of all, hope.

And who doesn't want that for another human being loved deeply and intimately by God?

. . . .

To Think About

What hard part of being a Christ-follower keeps you from sharing Him with others? What do you secretly doubt about God and what the Bible says about Him? Praying about and wrestling with doubts leads to deeper intimacy with and passion for Christ, but ignoring or pretending we don't have them can be detrimental to our own faith and the faith of people we love who don't know Him.

This week, when you get into bed, think of something you fully believe about God. Perhaps it's that He created the universe or that He loves your children. When I started doing this, it was much harder than I thought it would be. I quickly realized there were many things I didn't fully believe about God. I struggled at times to acknowledge that He worked all things out for the good of those who love Him. It was hard realizing that what I read in His Word, sang in church, and thought I believed were not deep, core beliefs in my heart. However, remember that moving to places of deeper beliefs about God, though difficult, is so much better than becoming complacent and stagnant in our faith.

Does Church Work?

"They devoted themselves to the apostles' teaching and to the fellowship, to the breaking of bread and to prayer."

Acts 2:42

Week Eight

My friends and I were talking about how the Christian life sometimes feels like two steps forward and fifty back. Although the Lord has helped free me from panic attacks, I still frequently worry about my kids. I recently spoke at a conference about how God has helped me stop people-pleasing, but I still spend too much time obsessing over my clothes, hair, and what others think of both. Even basic things like believing God's Word, loving unlikeable people, and driving nicely are ongoing struggles for me.

When I seem to consistently take fewer steps forward than back, I sometimes wonder if church works.

I know people who don't love Jesus who are patient, kind, and forgiving. They don't have road rage, and they aren't trying to look younger. Although I realize my perceptions of the unchurched may be just that, sometimes I still question. Sometimes I find myself preoccupied with my inabilities and failures, and I wonder. Sometimes I get stuck in cycles of doubt and skepticism about God and the Bible and I think to myself,

Does church make a colossal difference? Does it help me look any more like Jesus, really?

Last week, I read 2 Corinthians 4:16 for my weekly Bible study, and in the study, Pastor Matt Chandler reminded us to "win the day." He encouraged us not to beat ourselves up when we've already experienced God's grace and forgiveness, but to focus on being renewed today. For several days afterward, I woke up challenged and grateful for the simple reminder to ask the Spirit to help me quit looking back and instead just,

Win the Day.

A couple days after the Bible study, I met with my friend Eda to talk about ministry. When the conversation deviated to how difficult and worrisome it is to raise teenagers, my friend looked me square in the eyes, paused, and said assuredly,

"He'll redeem anything."

I walked away from that meeting with renewed confidence, peace, and a greater faith in God's plan for my children.

Later that week, at the transitional housing ministry where I volunteer, my friend Charles, who is a member there, shared a devotional. He asked, if we imagine our lives to be like living in a house made entirely of glass windows, why would we look only out of one? Why, when God has been teaching me so much this past year about His faithfulness, my identity in Him, and loving others, do I continue going back to the same window overlooking a view of doubt and defeat He's already upended? Charles reminded us of the power that comes when we,

Shift Our Focus.

Does church work? I'm realizing that it doesn't work as well for me when it's just my Sunday thing. My life and mind are fragmented, complicated, and distracted. I need daily Christian community, time in God's Word, and simple reminders. I need and love "Sunday church," but The Church is not a building, time slot, or activity. The Church works best when I live remembering that.

It's Christ at the center of who I am, what I do, and how I respond to the people and relationships in front of me,

Every day.

• • • •

To Think About

It's easier for me to "get my church on" all week because my job allows me a great deal of flexibility. Those who work full-time jobs in an office have to be more creative when it comes to being in Christian community and God's Word beyond Sunday morning. I have a friend who listens to sermons on her way to work. My husband reads the Bible on his phone every morning while eating his oatmeal before heading to the office. Another friend takes a trip with Christian girlfriends once a year for vacation.

If this seems too undesirable or difficult, pray and ask God this week to show you where, when, and how you can incorporate more of Him in a way that isn't overwhelming. He will show you if you keep asking!

Here's Your Sign

"So faith comes from hearing, and hearing through the word of Christ."

Romans 10:17 (ESV)

Week Nine

For a variety of reasons, this week was a rough week and I needed God to show up. Literally. I asked God, out loud, to send an angel, saint, or squirrel holding a sign—whatever—so I could sense His presence, be affirmed of His reality, and keep following Him passionately.

The irony of my request is that I don't believe in signs. Signs are things people see when they want confirmation of what they want. I'm not saying God never gives us signs, but generally speaking, I'm a skeptic.

But I also get tired.

Tired of persevering and waiting. Tired of writing, praying, and processing the same things over and over again. So, I asked for a sign I wanted, but knew I wouldn't get.

One of the things that made this week tough was struggling again with anxiety. Although God has freed me from the bondage of constant fear, worry is my default. I'm learning that I still need freedom from many control and anxiety issues (I'm also learning that those two things go hand-in-hand). My husband, not knowing the extent of my stressed-out week, was telling me about his Bible study and read Philippians 4 to me. Philippians 4:6-8 are my life verses. "Do not be anxious about anything, but in everything, by prayer and petition, with thanksgiving, present your requests to God. And the peace of God which transcends understanding, will guard your hearts and minds in Christ Jesus. Finally brothers, whatever is true, whatever is noble, whatever is right, whatever is pure, whatever is lovely, whatever is admirable—if anything is excellent or praiseworthy—think about such things." I have taught on Philippians 4:1-8 more than any other passage of Scripture in ten years of teaching the Bible. I know Philippians 4, but thank God, I listened intently as Chris read it.

The next morning, I woke up anxious. Instead of a seeing a sign reminding me that God is real, present, and all I hope and try to believe He is, I woke up stressed out with a pit in my stomach. Fortunately, Philippians 4 was fresh in my mind, so I started praying through it:

- "...with thanksgiving..." I thanked Him for my house, health, and husband.
- "...present your requests to God." I asked God to help me quit imagining the worst-case scenario endings to what I was worrying about.
- "Whatever is true..." I thanked God that nothing I was worrying about was a reality, but a "what-if."
- "Whatever is lovely..." I thanked Him for the beautiful day, my family, and my life.

And before I was finished getting ready for the day, I got my sign.

The sign wasn't delivered by flying monkey or Morgan Freeman. It wasn't big or bold, but quiet and effective. The sign came when I prayed His promises into my pain. A sense of His love and peace tangibly manifested itself when I slowed down long enough to hear His Word more loudly than the voices in my head.

Timothy Keller said, "Our prayers should arise out of immersion in the Scripture. [We] speak only to the degree we are spoken to...The wedding of the Bible and prayer anchors your life down in the real God." When I read, pray, and apply God's Word, I'm given more than a sign. I'm given peace, affirmation, and passion in real life to real problems, and I am reminded of the love of a very real God in a personal and intimate way.

....

To Think About

A woman at a conference was lamenting to me about struggles with anxiety, and I asked her if she knew Philippians 4:6-7. She not only knew it, she recited it verbatim. Hebrews 4:2 says, "For we also have had the gospel preached to us, just as they did, but the message they heard was of no value to them, because those who heard did not combine it with faith." Is there some Scripture that doesn't seem to "work" in your life? I know I feel that way sometimes. According to Hebrews, the problem isn't always that we don't know the verses, it's that we don't really believe what they say. I suggested to the woman at the conference to try to pray specifically through each line of Philippians 4:6-7 and personalize it the next time she was afraid. I encouraged her to actually present to God what she was afraid of, ask Him for what she hoped for in that moment, and thank Him for one thing even in that fear.

This week, pray through Philippians 4:6-8 if you are worried about something and also pray that God will help you believe more deeply the truth of His Word more and more. Because God loves us, He always wants to move us to deeper places of belief and trust in Him.

God's On My Side?

"The LORD your God is with you, he is mighty to save. He will take great delight in you, he will quiet you with his love, he will rejoice over you with singing."

Zephaniah 3:17

Week Ten

This Lenten holy week, I wanted to do something to think more about Jesus. I wanted to be intentional about concentrating on Christ's suffering, death, and resurrection, things I believe in profoundly, but rarely meditate on. After praying about it, I decided to do the one spiritual discipline I've done the least, hated the most, and felt is fanatic, outdated, and ascetic.

I fasted, and it was amazing.

Why was it amazing to have a terrible headache, think only about food (and barely about Jesus), and forgo eating when I didn't have to? After all, I gain no eternal reward by abstaining from my favorite foods.

Because this was the first time I had fasted since almost renouncing my faith.

In the past, I've tried fasting for various reasons. I've wanted an answer or a confirmation, or I've succumbed to the peer pressure of a corporate fast. I've fasted knowing Jesus fasted and said we should fast, or I've wanted to get something from a God who I viewed as powerful, punitive, and demanding.

Prior to last year, I struggled immensely with faith in a good and loving God. I wrestled for five years with doubt and apathy until I almost walked away from Christianity last year. Those very challenging and difficult-to-articulate years, however, eventually led me to a place where my faith in Christ finally moved from my brain deep into my heart, and I knew (not just mentally agreed to) God's crazy, non-sensical, passionate, unconditional love for me. I finally believed at the core of who I was that God was on my side, period. He's not on my side because I'm in seminary, teach women about the Bible, or have fasted (unsuccessfully) four or five times, but He's on my side when and because I swear, yell at my kids, eat Oreos, and deplore and defame drivers who don't use their signal on the highway.

How did I go from hating fasting to finding it amazing? When you know God is on your side and calls you to do things not because you have to, but because He has something for you, it changes everything. It turned my usual complaining into gratitude. It made me want to learn more about fasting instead of trying to find loopholes so I could eat. Yes, the first days of eating less to prepare for today's full fast came with its challenges (the headache, the desire to claw people's eyes out, etc.), but I can say what I've never said before about fasting.

I look forward to doing it again.

Lauren Winner, who converted from Judaism to Christianity, writes in her book *Mudhouse Sabbath*, "...I can begin to see that Jesus expects us to fast not because He is arbitrary or capricious or cruel, but because fasting does good work on both our bodies and our souls."[5] What has fasting this week taught me? When your heart knows you are completely known, fully loved, and that God is on your side, it changes you, body and soul.

· · · ·

[5] Winner, Lauren. *Mudhouse Sabbath*, 89. Brewster, MA: Paraclete Press, 2007.

To Think About

Take a minute to imagine what God looks like. Not necessarily His physical features, but how would you describe His demeanor and disposition? How about when you judge the lady sitting across the pew from you, covet your neighbor's new SUV, or cheat on your taxes? What is God's disposition toward you when you fail, lie, or worse?

Pastor Matt Chandler has a quote that has helped me begin to re-understand God's disposition toward me when I'm a disappointment to myself and those around me. "God is not in love with some future version of you. It's not you tomorrow that He loves and delights in. It's not you when you get your act together. If you believe that Christ's love for you is a future love for you, then you dismiss the cross of Christ."

This week, take time to think about how God sees you as you go about your day, the good, the bad, and the ugly.

I Am the Church

"Now you are the body of Christ and each one of you is a part of it."

1 Corinthians 12:27

Week Eleven

What is church to you? A building? A denomination? Hypocrites? Posers? People who love and care? People who are weak? People who think they are perfect? People who enforce, follow, and/or break rules? People who are fake? People who are kind? I am learning now more than ever that the church is all these things and more. Church is a complicated mix of good and bad, light and dark, love and hate. I know this about the church not because I've worked at a church, am a member at a church, or because I'm in seminary. I know the good, bad, and ugly about church because,

I am the church.

A normal day in my life begins with prayer on the treadmill. I ask God to help me be a better wife, then I go upstairs and criticize my husband about something petty. I ask God to help me be a more patient and wiser mom, and by the end of the day, I generally have at least one mothering regret or apology to make. I'll text my BFF a happy, kissy, heart-filled emoji, and then I'll give the lady driving slowly in the fast lane a look of condescending disgust when I fly past her on the freeway. I sometimes gossip, sometimes hate (though to justify it, I call it something nicer), and more than sometimes, I lose my temper. And those are just the things I'm willing to share that make up the imperfect, sinful, and dark side of me.

I am the church.

I also love Jesus. I pray for my favorite barista at Starbucks because she's awesome. I mentor an inner-city teenager. I prayed with my family at dinner for someone who was bullying one of my kids. I told my kids I wanted to claw the child's hair out, but that being a Christ-follower means obeying God's Word when it's hard. I volunteer at my kids' school and at church, and I repeatedly find myself providing housing for random foreign exchange students.

I am the church.

What I'm learning about church is that church is people. It is me and people like me: imperfect, trying-hard, Jesus-loving people who need a lot of grace, love, and prayer. What I'm learning about church is if I want it to look better, different, less hypocritical, and more like Jesus, there is only one thing to do.

Let God do His work in me.

. . . .

To Think About

Who or what is a struggle for you with church? Have you prayed about that issue and asked God what your part is in it (even if you think the problem has nothing to do with you)? My biggest and most consistent frustration with the church are the people in it.

This week, if there is someone in the church you find yourself easily annoyed with or jealous or critical of, tell God. When I find myself being critical, frustrated, or irritated with "the church," God eventually prompts me to pray in those hard places about the only person in the church that I can control. Myself. As depressing as that can be, I have experienced, over time, freedom and peace when I address only my part and my heart, even if the difficult person or situation I'm struggling with doesn't change. That, my sister, is His amazing grace at work!

Driving Slowly, in Jesus' Name

"Since we live by the Spirit, let us keep in step with the Spirit."

Galatians 5:25

Week Twelve

I love cars. I'm the middle child between two gearhead brothers. When other girls were playing "I Spy" on car rides, I was playing "Guess-the-Make-and-Model-of-that-Car-by-Looking-Only-at-the-Taillights-or-I'll-Hit-You." When I finally graduated from driving minivans a few years ago, I bought a cool, fast car. I felt I deserved it after carting my children around the world for twenty years. I was midlife and was entitled to my crisis.

Or so I thought.

Every year, I pray about what to forgo for Lent, and this year it was sweets. Since avoiding meat, dairy, and gluten due to my autoimmune issues this year, I've been compensating with sugar, the worst thing of all to ingest. So, I decided to say goodbye to dessert.

But yesterday, I heard that Spirit-inspired whisper I often talk about. How do I know it's the Spirit? I don't, but whenever I think of something I'd never come up with on my own and don't want to hear, I have a hunch it may be Spirit-inspired. Yesterday, the whisper wasn't about giving up sugar. It was about giving up driving like I'm Dale Earnhardt Jr.

Pastor Matt Chandler has a great analogy that illustrates why practicing spiritual disciplines like repentance and obedience aren't the same as trying to earn Christ's love and grace. Chandler, although having been married for more than a decade, still studies his wife. They still go on dates and retreats. Chandler doesn't do these things to get his wife to marry him, but to foster greater intimacy with her. Similarly, we don't read the Bible, go to church, or abstain from road rage to get Christ to love us. He already does. We're already in a covenant relationship with Christ, so although we don't have to do anything to be in that relationship, we read our Bible, spend time with Him, and forgo some things to deepen and grow our relationship with Him more and more.

I don't want to drive in comfort mode (where the imaginary monkeys who make my engine go are half asleep and have no work ethic). I don't want to drive the speed limit. That's wasting time. I childishly admit that I want to blow the doors off people who cut me off or drive like morons, but now I can't. I don't like that. However, listening to God isn't about personal sacrifice, punishment, or my desires.

It's about cultivating intimacy with Christ.

What I'm learning about people-pleasing, jealousy, and now driving aggressively is that people and cars aren't the problems. They're indicative of greater heart issues that God wants to free me from. When I remember that driving like an octogenarian isn't a punishment, it changes my attitude. When I can remind myself that driving the speed limit is meant to free me from other things I struggle with, my perspective shifts. And if I can remember that Christ died to give me abundant life apart from the car I drive, clothes I wear, and the mess I am, I will have gotten closer to getting the point of Lent.

. . . .

To Think About

What is an everyday, perpetual struggle for you? Driving fast, blowing your top, swearing, or maybe all of the above? Do you feel guilty when you do those things, or have you considered that God wants to free you from them because He loves you (more than you love your husband, kids, or morning cup of coffee)?

That kind of thinking doesn't come naturally to most of us, but this week, when the Spirit lovingly convicts you about that struggle, think about God's passionate and personal love for you and see if it changes anything.

Why I Like Arguing with My Husband

"If it is possible, as far as it depends on you, live at peace with everyone."

Romans 12:18

Week Thirteen

My husband and I have been arguing a lot, and I am so thankful.

I have loved Jesus for most of my married life, so I've prayed continuously to be a kinder, gentler, and more Christ-like wife to my husband, Chris. I have prayed to be a wife who responds without sarcasm and who uses a tone that sounds less like I'm Chris' kindergarten teacher and more like a woman who loves and respects her man. I've prayed all this and meant it.

The problem is that when the opportunity presents itself to look more like Jesus to my husband, I don't usually seize it. Although I want to be a nicer wife, I also subconsciously think/hope that because I've prayed about it, it should happen instantly, painlessly, and perhaps when I'm sleeping. Opportunities for me to be the wife I long to be present themselves all the time, but I've realized that I'm not often willing to do the work of dying to myself to become who I say I want to be.

So why am I happy about our recent arguments? Because I'm finally realizing that they're opportunities for me, when I least feel like it, to allow God to use me to answer my prayers. What does that look like? In our recent disagreements, it looks like stopping. When I've stopped to pray instead of defending myself, explaining how I was right, and ensuring I was thoroughly and completely heard, this question came into my little Asian head:

What's your part in this?

God has not allowed me to justify my feelings or wallow in my hurt. He has not given me permission to complain about Chris or justify why I had to use that tone or those words. God has not said, "Let's focus on what Chris needs to do differently next time." He has only asked me what I need to change, do differently, or apologize for, and although that's about as much fun as algebra or having the stomach flu, it's how God is transforming me slowly into the wife I've wanted to be for twenty-five years.

Do I think it's fair that I must only deal with "my part" in a fight involving two imperfect people? No. But it has been in that place of injustice that I have found less frustration, more joy, and greater peace by focusing on the only person in this relationship that I have any control over. Not only can I not change Chris, I have enough to work on when I look only at "my part." I have been humbled enough to see how my self-centeredness and struggle to see myself as Christ does spills over into our relationship and hurts the man I love so deeply.

In focusing only on my part, I'm also overwhelmed with the gift of Christ's grace in my life. I am forgiven. I am deeply known and loved, despite when I fall short. When we ask God to transform us and then look for opportunities to be transformed, we can't help but become changed.

Gratitude has a way of doing that.

• • • •

To Think About

When you're in conflict with someone else, have you ever asked yourself, "What's my part?" It feels very uncomfortable, undesirable, and unjust. You won't like it or want to continue asking it, but I believe that's where the Lord does some of His best work in me. Do you want a deeper faith? A better marriage? To look more like Jesus?

Try praying "what's my part?" this week if you find yourself in a disagreement, and then start listening.

Burning My AARP Card

"Because of the LORD's great love we are not consumed, for his compassions never fail. They are new every morning; great is your faithfulness. I say to myself, 'The LORD is my portion; therefore I will wait for him.'"

Lamentations 3:22-24

Week Fourteen

I'm not sure if it was the AARP cards that arrived in the mail, my son's upcoming graduation, or my ever-aging hormones, but I'm struggling. Struggling with some relational losses, my nest emptying, and not knowing what's coming for me in this next season of life.

I'm struggling.

I remember when my youngest child started kindergarten. I cried for two weeks. I cried when my oldest child started high school and when she left for college. I've been crying on and off all year knowing my son Casey will be leaving soon too, and the minute he leaves, my youngest will have his car and be far, far away from her Smother. As much as I understand that these are inevitable changes,

I'm in a funk.

Although no one has died, I'm not sick, and from all outward appearances, my life is good (and it is), I'm not. Sometimes our reality is our reality and we can't wish or rationalize hurt away. If it were that easy, I'd be out burning my AARP card or something else fun and productive.

Instead, for the past twenty-four hours, I've cried, journaled, and binge-watched chick flicks. I texted a friend, talked to my husband, and have taken a lot of aspirin. I haven't dealt with these kinds of emotions for longer than I can remember, and I just want them to go away.

Now.

It occurred to me while working out and praying this morning that in my funk, I'd failed to do what I've taught and reminded my kids and the women I speak to at conferences, ad nauseam. I'd failed to practice what I preach and live out what should be my default by now. Not only had I failed to pray and read my Bible in my hurt, it hadn't even crossed my mind. When I reflected on why that was, I realized it was because I wanted a quick fix to the putridness. I wanted the ache to leave.

Now.

But today I realized that I have to, once again, cling to my cactus. Clinging to our cactus is the intentional act of sitting with our pain and talking to God about it. It's not wishing for the pain to leave or for a quick solution. It's choosing to remain in the uncomfortable space until God speaks, teaches, or moves.

What's the point, advantage, or benefit of clinging to what hurts? When I text friends, talk to my husband, or call my mom with my problems, the advice is well-intended and nominally helpful, but people, even our closest people, don't know our hearts. The advantage of waiting on God in our suffering is that His answers are intimate. Personal. Specific. His solutions meet me in exactly the way I need (even though He's usually incredibly slow in delivering those answers).

If you need me, I'll be with my cactus. I don't need sympathy, essential oils, or a well-intended Scripture verse, but I will take your prayers. And I'll be okay. For the first time in a while, I believe that to be true.

. . . .

To Think About

What are you struggling with right now? How much time have you spent praying about it? Even if you don't feel like praying, will you commit to praying about that struggle every day this week?

Sometimes I think I fail to pray because I'm upset with God, afraid of His answer, or worse, afraid He won't answer at all. Whatever the emotions and fear, share your heart honestly and openly with the Lord. Right now. Then do it again tomorrow and the next day. You've got nothing to lose and everything to gain.

Social Media Sabbatical

"Stop trusting in mere humans,
who have but a breath in their nostrils.
Why hold them in esteem?"

Isaiah 2:22

Week Fifteen

I've often thought about what it means to have a Sabbath. Even though I've been a Christian for twenty years, this notion is daunting and undesirable. But recently, in an attempt to have some kind of Sabbath, I began abstaining from social media on Sundays.

For some, this wouldn't be hard, but it was for me. But it was also freeing.

When I took a picture of our family at the Packer game and couldn't post it, I became grateful. Grateful I didn't have to spend time trying to find a picture I looked satisfactory in or thinking of a comment that was witty, but not boastful. When I couldn't post pictures of my kids and their friends decorating our Christmas tree one Sunday, I remembered a friend who didn't have the room, time, or finances for a tree, and I became thankful that I wouldn't make my friend feel sad, jealous, or otherwise. I also realized that I spend too much mental energy on social media that I could spend on other things, people, and time with the Lord.

Then there was my blog.

Readership on my blog had recently dropped. Although God is teaching me how to hear what He says about me more loudly than the lies I often tell myself (I'm a bad writer, I've nothing to say, etc.), when my readership dropped, I began rereading my posts and hyper-focusing on my blog statistics and comments.

I began questioning, debating, and contemplating what I could do, control, and change. I prayed about discontinuing my blog. And that's when I realized something else that has made me decide to take a social media sabbatical, indefinitely.

I was finding my worth, defining my purpose, and getting life from stats, hits, and likes.

One of the reasons I joined my discipleship group last year was to quit people-pleasing. Although I've learned so much and come a long way, I'm realizing that I'm still trying to please people instead of one Person.

I don't want to leave social media, and I'm not going to completely. But I'm tired. Tired of wishing I'd quit caring what people think of me but constantly checking social media. I'm tired of spending hours on my phone wishing I was spending it with my family, writing, or doing something else that had eternal value, but not doing anything to make that happen.

Goodbye, social media. I'll miss you, but God doesn't call us to obedience to torture us. Out of His love, He calls us to things because He wants better for us. Remembering that is already making my sabbatical easier, purpose-filled, and more freeing.

• • • •

To Think About

I didn't think likes and comments on social media were helping me feel better about myself until I prayed and thought about it more deeply and intentionally. Many of my friends aren't on social media very often, if at all, but if you are, have you ever taken a week-, month-, or year-long sabbatical? Does the idea of such a break make you uncomfortable, like it did for me? If so, are you willing this week to pray about taking a break and seeing what you learn?

Why the Bible is Confusing

"This is what the LORD says, he who appoints the sun to shine by day, who decrees the moon and stars to shine by night, who stirs up the sea so that its waves roar—the LORD Almighty is his name."

Jeremiah 31:35

Week Sixteen

I was recently listening to a podcast about how God speaks to us. The facilitators said that we hear from God by reading the Bible, which isn't meant to be difficult. They also said that God doesn't give answers in Scripture that are too hard to understand or are "murky." Although I love God, read my Bible almost daily, and rely on my faith in Christ to do life, sometimes I do find the Bible confusing, complicated, and seemingly contradictory. Sometimes I find it murky. So once again, as I listened to something I sort of believed, I found myself asking God to help my unbelief.

Later that day, I was thinking about my recent trip to China. When people asked me how it was, I always struggled to respond. How could I give words to describe how it felt to walk on the Great Wall of China with my children? How could I explain the relationships we forged with our hosts who did not speak English but showered us with unspoken thoughtfulness and love? How could I share the emotions I had looking into the broken and abandoned eyes of children at the orphanage we toured? What words could adequately describe how it felt when one of the orphans gave me a warm, spontaneous, lingering hug before we left?

Similarly, when people asked me how I liked the Grand Canyon last spring, words like "amazing," "incredible," and "awesome" seemed trite, cliché, and ambiguous. Language cannot convey the incomprehensible magnitude and awe of the Grand Canyon. Mere adjectives cannot give justice to that which is bigger than we are and more beautiful and indescribable than language can illustrate. Words are inadequate. They can be beautiful, deep, and expressive, but they are also incomplete and insufficient.

God doesn't mean to make the Bible complicated or confusing. He isn't trying to make us work hard to unpack it to prove our devotion, dedication, or love. He isn't trying to muddy the waters of our understanding. But He is God, and I am not. If words cannot describe the Grand Canyon, how can they describe and adequately explain the One who made it?

The more time I spend reading the Bible, confusing, difficult, and murky as it sometimes seems, the more I am learning to respect how big God is. I cannot grasp an infinitesimal amount of His magnitude, nor can words sufficiently or adequately describe His power, beauty, and love. The more I wrestle with what I struggle to believe, the more God seems to reveal Himself in a way I can understand.

Not because He has to, but because He wants to.

. . . .

To Think About

What do you do when you come across something in the Bible that seems confusing or is something you cannot believe (i.e. a talking donkey, a pregnant virgin, or a sea parting)? Do you ignore it? Rationalize it? Wonder about it then forget it? The next time you struggle to believe something in God's Word, ask God about it.

Charles Spurgeon said, "Some of us who have preached the Word for years, and have been the means of working faith in others and of establishing them in the knowledge of the fundamental doctrines of the Bible, have nevertheless been the subjects of the most fearful and violent doubts as to the truth of the very gospel we have preached." Everyone experiences doubt about the Bible, but the wise among us will not abandon or ignore those doubts.

This week, pursue and pray through your doubts and don't stop until God moves you to a greater belief in Him.

When Faith Works

"It is well with my soul."

Horatio Spafford

Week Seventeen

Not long ago, I found out that my friend has leukemia. I haven't talked to my friend for several valid reasons (I was in China, she's been in and out of the hospital, etc.), but I realized that there is another reason I haven't talked to her.

I lost my grandma to leukemia.

I was too little to remember many details, but I wasn't too little to remember my mom flying with my little brother to Japan to visit my grandma for the last time. I wasn't too little to be sad when I saw my mom crying many times when she came back. Although that was over forty years ago and medical advances have come far since then, I'm scared for my friend Karol.

But she isn't.

When talking to a mutual friend last week, I didn't ask how Karol was. She'd been feeling awful for a few months, and she'd been in and out of doctor and chemotherapy appointments. I could surmise how she "was." I instead asked our friend something I knew she understood and could answer. I asked how Karol's soul was.

We want our faith to sustain us when we get sick, lose someone, or are afraid. We want the Bible verses we've memorized, the songs we've sang, and the things we've taught our kids to actually hold up when the rug gets pulled out. What I wanted to know about Karol, my friend and mentor, was if it was well with her soul, even though it wasn't well with her body.

"Her soul is amazing."

Not only is her soul amazing, my friend said that Karol never wants to go back to life before leukemia. God was teaching Karol so much, and it was awesome. And although I would have expected all of this from Karol, since her faith was so strong, inspiring, and solid before she was sick, I was so incredibly relieved to hear her faith in Christ was not only holding her up, it was ridiculously, supernaturally, and unexplainably allowing her to thrive.

When trouble comes, I want to be like Karol. I want my soul to be amazing. I want to look back at hard times like my other friend Cindy did once she was cancer-free. Cindy told me, with tears in her eyes, that she missed the intimacy and connectedness she had with Christ when she was sick. And in the case of both of these amazing women, they would tell you that it was the often difficult and mundane daily discipline of knowing Christ's love personally and intimately through prayer and time in His Word, that sustained them in the unimaginable.

How is Karol doing? Better than most of us who are physically well. Better, because her Hope does not disappoint. Better, because when by all accounts it shouldn't be, it is truly, *well with her soul.*

• • • •

To Think About

What do you think when you hear about people like Karol? I used to think that people were crazy when they would say, "Cancer was a blessing." Do you fear the unthinkable happening, or do you ask God to help continue to move you to a place where your faith is unshakable, no matter what? I believe, and have seen in friends like Karol and Cindy, that the small, daily steps we take toward God in prayer, being in His Word, and surrounding ourselves in Christian community are creating in us greater resiliency, faith, and strength.

This week, read your Bible when you don't feel like it, turn off your radio on your way to work so you can pray, and have coffee with that wise woman who sits in the pew across from you. Proverbs 30:5 says, "Every word of God is flawless; he is a shield to those who take refuge in him." Thanks be to God that He is our shield when we need Him most. Let's take refuge in Him every day!

When The Church Fails. Again.

"Let the peace of Christ rule in your hearts, since as members of one body you were called to peace."

Colossians 3:15a

Week Eighteen

When I learned recently that the second pastor at my church in six months resigned due to marital infidelity, I was broken, angry, and arrogant. I was sad for another devastated young family. I was angry because I had to tell my kids...again. I was arrogant, not because I had questions, but because I felt I deserved answers.

I went to church the night we received the announcement about our pastor. My friend, who leads our youth, invited me to pray over the students' Wednesday night service. I wanted to do something. I wanted to go for her, my kids, and the other kids who would be there. So, I showed up to help others, but instead ended up being the one receiving it.

Although I prayed for my friend's teaching, the brave team leading worship, and the students, I was broken and angry. I had fought back tears all night for our church, our pastor's family, and my kids. A friend met me to pray that night too, but when she started talking about how we all sin, I wasn't feeling it. I am pretty open about my struggles with profanity, judgment, and anger, but multiple affairs from our teaching pastor?

I couldn't reconcile that.

As I began to pray over the youth service, however, the Spirit began whispering to me. He began meeting me in my hurt, anger, and desire for answers. He met me in and despite my brokenness, pain, and prideful heart.

The first thing the Lord reminded me that night was that regardless of what happens in this life, God is still everything His Word tells us He is. He is active in our lives and teaches and helps us in temptations, but we still have a choice. When I chose to take the Jesus sticker off my car because I drive like an idiot, it did not negate God's goodness. When my pastor fails, God's power, love, and authority remains perfect and wholly intact.

The second thing I learned is that I don't need answers to my pastor's problems. Last time I checked, I'm still struggling with being a defensive wife, an angry mother, and worse than I care to admit. To the best of my knowledge, I'm still only in charge of me, and I have enough issues to worry about to last a lifetime. I also realized that night that not only did I not need answers, knowing them would not change anything for me or anyone else.

Lastly, I relearned not to ask "Why?" but "What now?" What am I going to do to support my church now? What can I do to serve now? What am I going to pray now? After Peter had denied Christ three times, Jesus did not ask Peter why he failed. He told him to feed God's sheep. He asked, essentially, "What now, Peter?"

When we move past "Why" to "What now," we can move away from paralysis and onto productivity. When we can shift our focus away from our own pain, we can start to focus on the brokenness of others. We can begin to move toward a renewed sense of our dependence on God personally and corporately.

When we seek God out and He meets us in our brokenness, pain, and pride,

We can move.

• • • •

To Think About

Is there something or someone in your church that you struggle to understand, agree with, or forgive? Have you spent dedicated and prolonged time praying and reading the Bible about that struggle? If you haven't, are you willing to this week?

As someone who has been in ministry for twenty years, I have had my share of hurt, disappointment, and frustration with the church, but when I've finally prayed and sought God out in those hard places, He always reveals a solution. The answer always addresses my heart, pride, hurt, and response, and although that doesn't change anyone or anything else, it has allowed me to continue to be the church with peace, forgiveness, and greater intimacy with and sustenance in Christ.

Spirit-Inspired Whispers

"Anything of spiritual significance that happens in your life will be a result of God's activity in you. He is infinitely more concerned with your life and your relationship with Him than you or I could possibly be."

Henry Blackaby

Week Nineteen

Several weeks ago, I was praying as I often do, early in the morning. I walked over to open the blinds and saw someone walking their dog. Because we have a corner lot, I often catch people letting their dogs relieve themselves in my yard without cleaning up their deposits. If there's one thing that annoys me more than slow drivers in the fast lane, it's landmines in my yard. So I watched and waited.

That's when I heard, "Look Away."

I kept looking out the window until I heard it again. "Look Away." The problem was, I didn't really want to look away. I wanted to watch. I wasn't going to do anything but seethe, complain, and harbor animosity toward them for twenty minutes, but it was almost impossible to look away. When I finally did look away, I realized that I had no idea if my neighbor cleaned up after Fido. I couldn't seethe, complain, or harbor animosity, and that was the point.

"Look Away" gave me peace and helped me love my neighbor.

I didn't just "Look Away" from the landmine incident. For weeks, I kept hearing "Look Away." When my husband was doing something that I would normally have corrected or "helped" him do better (something colossal like using the wrong dish towel), rather than belittle and disrespect him, I heard, "Look Away."

"Look Away" helped me nag Chris one less time about something that didn't really matter in the big scheme of things.

When I thought I overheard someone saying something derogatory about how one of my kids played in basketball, I heard "Look Away" again. I would never confront them, but I would harbor anger and hatred toward them (even though I would smile and make pleasantries to their face). When I heard "Look Away," I became calm enough to pray and decided that maybe I hadn't even heard them correctly.

"Look Away" helped me give someone the benefit of the doubt.

When my kids were driving across the state and I wanted to check my stalker app every five minutes to make sure they were okay, God reminded me again to "Look Away." Instead of constantly looking at my phone and checking the clock, I enjoyed a canoe ride and walk with my husband.

"Look Away" helped me enjoy the people in front of me that day instead of being consumed by fear over something I couldn't control anyway.

How do I know God told me to "Look Away"? After all, "Look Away" isn't rocket science. It isn't a deep theological truth unearthed by hours of Bible reading and meditation. Morgan Freeman in a white suit did not show up in my office and tell me to "Look Away."

Outside of Scripture, we cannot know with absolute certainty that the Lord told us something, however, I have a sense that the Lord prompted me to "Look Away." I believe it was a Spirit-inspired whisper because it has been an answer to my almost daily prayers to love my neighbor, experience more peace, and be a nicer wife. I think God whispered those words into my little Asian head because, unlike most things, it's stuck, has allowed me to do life differently, and is helping me live with less regret.

How do we hear God?

By praying and being in His Word continually, then listening carefully for His merciful whisper in the mundane but meaningful moments of our day.

· · · ·

To Think About

When you pray about something, do you actively expect and look for God to respond? It was said of Dietrich Bonhoeffer that, "he did not hope that God heard his prayers, but knew it."[6] That is both frightening and challenging to me. If I'm honest, I don't think I want God to answer nearly as much as I want Him to answer the way I want Him to answer.

This week, let's listen to ourselves pray and discern if our heart and mind are praying and believing that God hears us!

[6] Metaxas, Eric. *Bonhoeffer: Pastor, Martyr, Prophet, Spy*, 237. Nashville: Thomas Nelson, 2010.

My
Murderous Rage

"Why do you look at the speck of sawdust
in your brother's eye and pay no attention
to the plank in you own eye?"

Matthew 7:3

Week Twenty

In her book, *The Hiding Place*, Corrie ten Boom talks about "murderous rage," the immense, all- consuming fury she felt toward the Nazi Germans who imprisoned and tortured her and her family, and who eventually killed her sister and father during World War II.

Sadly, I've also experienced murderous rage. I would have never called it that, of course. I would never want to hurt anyone, let alone murder them. Yes, I get upset at times, but murderous rage? Ever since I read ten Boom's book, however, I started paying more attention to my anger. I realized that, at times, the depth of my hostility minimally borders on murderous rage. Unfortunately, my profound and violent indignation wasn't directed at hate-filled Nazis.

It was toward Christians.

If random people verbally attack me or my family or if I see something on the internet blaspheming Christians, I don't have murderous rage. I may get annoyed, cynical, or upset, but it's easier for me to accept and legitimize hurtful words if people don't profess to follow Christ. However, when people who call themselves Christians, who faithfully attend churches where grace and truth are taught, act or speak in a way that doesn't seem even remotely "Christian," that's when the gloves come off, particularly if said words and actions are directed toward one of my kids.

Recently, one of my children was being bullied by a church-going peer, and murderous rage rose up in me like a tsunami. My ears, head, and stomach felt like they were on fire. I literally shook and had the urge to strike something or someone. Once the physical manifestations of my anger subsided, I tried to pray; however, it's almost impossible for me to pray for someone whose behavior I can't understand or explain because I think, they should know better.

I continued trying to pray about my murderous rage. I knew it was wrong and irrational. I knew it wasn't what Christ would do. But sometimes it's incredibly hard to un-feel hostility you feel entirely justified having.

However, not long after this incident, one of my Christian mentors, unaware of my dilemma, told me she'd also been upset with someone for acting unchristian. But after she prayed about it for many weeks, she sensed the Lord reminding her that other Christ-followers are authentically where they are. Every Christian is genuinely—to the best of their ability, understanding, and humanness—doing their best to love and follow God. Five years ago, I didn't know or feel the depth of Christ's love for me like I do now. And I could not have realized it faster, been told to experience it sooner, or understood it more quickly. Believe me, I tried. Every Christian is at a different place in their faith journey.

We are all authentically where we are.

Has this timely reminder allowed me to stop desiring to strangle Christians who I think are mean and should know better? Have I been able to pray blessings upon those who, by all appearances, intentionally say and do unkind and hurtful things to my kids?

No.

But it's helped.

When the Spirit reminds me that Christians are "authentically where we are," it has helped me pause. And when I pause, I remember that I sometimes act wholly unchristian, even when I know better. When I pause, the Spirit prompts me to pray, and in that, helps me remember thoughtless, insensitive things I do and have done, with or without realizing it. When I remember we are all authentically where we are, I can minimally whisper a half-hearted prayer, asking God to help me love instead of hate. When I pause, the wave of murderous rage inside me doesn't get so big, overwhelm me as long, and doesn't leave the carnage it has in the past.

And when I pause, I see God giving me an opportunity to slowly start replacing my murderous rage with humility and gratitude for His grace that finds me authentically where I am. Every day.

. . . .

To Think About

I wrote this reflection about six months before editing it to include in this devotional. When I was rereading it, I was reminded about the person I had directed my murderous rage toward. I was also convicted to stop working and pray for that person. When I did, I was reminded that in the name of protecting and loving my own child, I had intentionally chosen to dismiss the fact that this person was a teenager. I was also reminded of a friend who had bravely just apologized to me for something hurtful she had done. Lastly, I was prompted to not only pray for this person but write them an apology.

Is there anyone in the family of God you have had murderous rage toward? Or perhaps you aren't as violent and unstable as I am. Maybe you've just been really angry or upset at someone.

Regardless of the level of your hostility, pray for that person this week. If you find yourself unwilling or unable to pray, then pray about that. Pray every day this week (and longer, if needed) to see what God wants to free you from in that relationship. I've been learning firsthand that unforgiveness is a burden and weight that God not only wants to free us from, but when we seek His help, He also equips us to be able to forgive.

How to Love in the Controversial

"This is love: not that we loved God, but that he loved us and sent his Son as an atoning sacrifice for our sins. Dear friends, since God so loved us, we also ought to love one another."

1 John 4:11

Week Twenty-One

It's hard being a Christian.

If I believe and try to follow the Bible—what I learn in church and may even feel passionately about—the reality is that I don't usually know how or have the confidence to live it out. What does it look like to love my friend who's a lesbian? What constitutes condoning or critiquing? How do I speak up for the unborn? If I write a post about abortion, my pro-life friends will love it and my pro-choice friends will hate it. I've polarized instead of proselytized.

"Love God and Love People," the t-shirt says. How? How do I love and follow God and His Word without making people feel like I'm judging, hating, or thinking I'm better than they are?

I have no idea.

But these people and things matter to me. I love my friend who is gay. We've cried together because she's been hurt by Christians. I've cried and lamented to her because I can't pick and choose the parts of the Bible that are easy—for me or for her. I cringed when I read that a leading cause of death in the U.S. is abortion. Although I have close friends I love who have had abortions, I cannot reconcile, reason, or rationalize that statistic.

I believe in the core of my soul that I will give an account to God for my life, actions, and words, or lack thereof, someday. What will I say?

I have no idea.

I recently read about a man who wanted to help an acquaintance who was going through something terrible. He wanted to help in a big way, but for various legitimate reasons, he couldn't. He wanted to be a "stretcher-bearer," but couldn't. So, he did what he could do. He did something.

He carried the Band-Aids.

I have no idea how to be a Billy Graham or a Mother Teresa kind of Christian. I lack confidence and knowledge. I can't field big questions or spiritual controversies. I can't be an EMT, but I can definitely carry Band-Aids.

I can continue being a friend to my friend who's gay. She's easy to love, and although I don't always know what to say or do where we don't agree, I don't have to. That's God's part. My part is to bring Band-Aids, and I can't do that if I don't show up.

I just started volunteering at a pregnancy clinic in Milwaukee that cares about forging relationships with women who are pregnant, afraid, and confused. I'm also going to keep praying for the unborn, doctors, and state and federal elected officials on both sides of the issues.

Following Jesus isn't as hard as I've made it, I suppose. It's as easy as doing something small to love people. It's more about doing than saying. It's as easy as bringing Band-Aids to the hurting instead of banners to a cause. It's as easy as showing up where the Lord calls us to the people He puts in front of us.

After all, that's what Jesus did.

• • • •

To Think About

Where can you bring Band-Aids to the people and situations that are in front of you this week? Do you work, volunteer, or frequent places where you are uncomfortable sharing your faith? Do you interface with people who are different than you in color, political affiliation, or faith? What Band-Aids can you bring, in the name of love, to the people right in front of you this week?

Intolerance of Doughheads

"If you love those who love you, what reward will you get? Are not even the tax collectors doing that? And if you greet only your own people, what are you doing more than others? Do not even pagans do that?"

Matthew 5:46-47

Week Twenty-Two

The other day, we went shopping with Foley (the teen we've been mentoring for the last three years) and he was his usual exuberant (hyper) self. Although Foley has endured an unthinkable childhood, he is truly one of the most joyful, thankful individuals I know. Foley doesn't smile, he lights up a room. He doesn't say hello, he exudes love. Foley doesn't stand in lines, he bounces.

A man next to us in line didn't appreciate Foley's bounce. Although Foley wasn't interfering with him, he kept glaring at Foley. Every dirty look made me want to smack the guy. When I got in the car fuming, I thought that I should pray for the man. Not because I wanted to or because he deserved it, but because we're supposed to pray for our enemies. So, I prayed a half-hearted, reluctant prayer that I didn't mean.

I was mad at the man because he had no idea. No idea that Foley was removed from his home due to egregious neglect and abuse when he was little. No idea that Foley's sister eventually got adopted but he didn't. That horrible, insensitive man had no idea that Foley has lived most of his life in group homes with no parents, family, or anyone else advocating for him. I didn't give it any conscious thought, but I knew my anger toward this doughhead was legitimate and justified.

I have thought about this guy several times since then. I asked my husband if he saw the man's judgmental glances. I told a friend about him and how I reluctantly prayed for him. Subconsciously, I guess I was pretty proud of myself for praying, not realizing how insidious my pride, hypocrisy, and judgment were disguising themselves in my heart and mind.

Romans 2:1 says, "You, therefore, have no excuse, you who pass judgment on someone else, for at whatever point you judge another, you are condemning yourself, because you who pass judgment do the same things." Being the "good Christian" I am, I've memorized that verse. I've taught on it, and I've even been convicted by it before (multiple times, in fact). Yet in judging someone I had no idea about, I was not being very "good" or Christ-like at all. Now who's the doughhead?

Why do I need to ask God to reveal my hidden sins every day? It's not so I can be forgiven. Christ already took care of that. It's because when the Spirit reveals and weeds out the places I grieve Him, I can better honor and thank Jesus for what He did at the cross. I can become aware of sins I would otherwise rationalize, call something else, and feel entitled to have. I can love those Christ died for instead of subconsciously continuing to harbor anger and hatred for them because I have reasoned they deserve it, when I have no idea.

Although it's embarrassing and humbling to realize our hidden, "justified" sins, when we do, we can live and love more like Jesus, and in doing so, we can extend to others some of the love and grace that's been given to us.

· · · ·

To Think About

There have been times I have thought about Romans 2:1 and reasoned I would never do (fill-in-the-blank). I have rationalized that I would never do whatever offense, accusation, or hurtful thing someone has done to me. However, the point of Romans 2 is to remind us that we have no idea. We have no idea what another person is thinking, how they've been hurt, and the places where they may be instinctively and subconsciously protecting themselves. We cannot know another person's heart, only God can.

I am learning firsthand that sometimes the way we pray for and forgive others who are acting in a way we cannot understand is, in part, simply obedience. Christ has forgiven me, and I am called to forgive others seven times seventy times. Whether or not I agree, can rationalize, or even feel like forgiving someone, we are called to follow suit after the forgiveness Christ has given us. I'm struggling to forgive someone in my life right now, but with every new offense, regardless of their lack of contrition and my own feelings, I am continuing to ask God to help me remember and live out love that is patient, kind, and that keeps no record of wrong.

This week, ask God to help you forgive someone who has wronged, hurt, or snubbed you. Forgiveness, I'm learning, is a process. But I'm also learning that the process does get easier the more we pray, dig into Scripture about forgiveness, and obey, whether we feel like it or not.

I Can't Tell Them That

"...your Father knows what you need before you ask him."

Matthew 6:8b

Week Twenty-Three

Not long ago, I prepared for the most stressful teaching I've given all year. Although I've spoken to groups of hundreds of women this year, the group of sixteen attendees I was going to teach this time was the most difficult and pressure-filled yet. After praying, fasting, writing, rewriting, begging, and then getting extremely frustrated, I came up with exactly nothing. I asked God repeatedly what I was supposed to teach, but...

He seemed silent.

I was admittedly annoyed. God knew I had been praying for weeks about what to share with these sixteen individuals. He knew my desperation and complete dependency on Him. He knew I needed Him, yet when I went to bed the night before I was supposed to teach to these sixteen students at the Milwaukee Rescue Mission high school, I had no idea what I was going to say.

Because I'm currently writing about the lives of the homeless in Milwaukee for grad school, I've heard firsthand what it's like to grow up without. I've heard what can happen when you grow up without parents, a home, or stability. I'm learning how dark, awful, and desperate it is to be without basic things that I take for granted. After praying about all of this for several days, I asked God in lieu of those stories, "How?" As I made my bed, I wondered, "How can I tell them Jesus loves them?"

How can I tell children who have been abused, neglected, or

are homeless that Jesus loves them? How can I tell kids whose parents may have abandoned them that Jesus loves them? How can I talk to them about God, the Bible, and mercy as a privileged, wealthy, Amerasian who's never ever been without? I kept asking and genuinely wanted God to tell me.

"How do I tell them You love them?"

And in the mundane moments of making my bed, after my pious and aesthetic attempts to hear God and the frustration that accompanied not only His silence, but the feeling I'd wasted so much time trying to hear from Him with nothing to show for it in the end, I heard a thought so loudly in my head that it stopped me dead in my tracks:

"How can you not tell them I love them?"

Sometimes when I'm trying to hear God, what I really want is an easy answer, a quick fix, a formula. I thought I wanted God to give me a message to help or encourage these kids, but God knew that wasn't what they needed. They needed, regardless of my words, to hear, know, and be convinced that I believed what I was saying.

God never told me what He wanted me to share with the sixteen high schoolers that day. He didn't give me a passage, topic, or illustration. What He gave me instead was what I had been asking Him for all along. He gave me what they needed by giving me what I needed. A much-needed reminder that His love always matters and is the only hope any of us really has.

• • • •

To Think About

When you ask God for something, do you already have in mind what the answer should be? It's difficult for me to ask the Lord something and not try and lend my advice. It's hard for me to leave answers up to Him and wait.

This week, when you ask for something in prayer, perhaps also pray for the patience and faith to trust His timing and response!

Losing my [Thick] Head

"Pride goes before destruction,
a haughty spirit before a fall."

Proverbs 16:18

Week Twenty-Four

Today, I'm hosting a party for my book, *Walking By the Homeless*. Although I'm an extrovert and love seeing my friends, I'm dreading the party. Why?

Although part of me craves being the center of attention, another part of me loathes it.

I'm embarrassed when people ask me face-to-face about the book. I've rolled my eyes (figuratively) when people have said that they're proud of me. When I confided this to my close friend, she said that if one of my kids or friends had written a book, I would be thrilled and wouldn't hesitate to praise them. She also told me out of love and concern that she's noticed my struggle to accept compliments. And she was right. There is a pervasive voice in my heart and head that is critical and condemning. I told my friend that I needed to continue praying about all of this, things I already knew and have been praying and lamenting over in my discipleship group with her every week for months.

Yesterday, I drove into the inner city to pray. I went to Hope Street, a ministry where I volunteer that provides transitional living for the formerly incarcerated, homeless, or addicted. I didn't know why I felt drawn to go, but I knew it was where I was supposed to be. Mr. Wiggins, a 70-year-old man who lives at Hope Street, prayed and asked God to help us each find a way to be an encouragement to someone, and then he said,

"Lord, help us not be too thickheaded that we cannot accept encouragement from someone else."

A little while later, another member was talking about how grateful she was to live at Hope Street. She talked how she couldn't see her husband because he'd broken twelve of her ribs and punctured her lung "with one blow." She said her daughter saw it happen, then started talking about her history of drug abuse, but stopped suddenly. She paused for a very long time, then said,

"But, I'm not looking back there. I'm looking ahead."

After another pause, she talked about how much she's changed since coming to Hope Street. She said she could hear God so clearly now that she isn't on drugs. She talked about how good she feels and again about how thankful she was.

As I always do when I attend prayer at Hope Street, I learned some things yesterday. I learned that I have the choice to receive or reject encouragement. The latter seems quite foolish and "thickheaded" when we realize that it is a choice. The second thing I learned is that condemnation is a thief. Believing the lies I tell myself about myself robs me of seeing God, others, and myself under the light of reality. I also learned that I can't hear or receive love from others when I'm focused on feeling bad about myself.

I learned most of all that whenever I catch myself condemning myself, I need to remember,

I'm not looking back there. I'm looking ahead.

· · · ·

To Think About

Is it hard for you to receive compliments? It is for most women I know. Have you ever tried just saying thank you when someone compliments you, and nothing else? I have said thank you, but then made a joke demeaning my efforts, talents, or otherwise. It's hard to just say thank you, but let's not be too thickheaded to receive encouragement today.

This week, practice saying thank you when someone compliments you. If that's hard or you just can't do it, ask God why that is. Then listen, look, and wait to find out what He shows you.

Scary Prayers

"For the grace of God has appeared that offers salvation to all people. It teaches us to say 'No' to ungodliness and worldly passions, and to live self-controlled, upright, and godly lives in this present age."

Titus 2:11-12

Week Twenty-Five

Recently, when I was praying, I had an awful thought. I was going to be attending a funeral later in the day, so I prayed that God would help me look like Christ to my family and anyone else I'd encounter that afternoon. What a noble and inspired request.

That's when I had the horrific thought. Rather than ask God to help me look like Christ, why not pray for opportunities to act and speak in front of those friends and family in a way that would shine Christ's light?

Insert barf emoji.

As I often do when I don't like what God says to me, I ignored the thought. It was too convicting, too frightening, and required me to do more than I was comfortable doing. Most people already think I'm weird and too "religious." The thought of asking God to give me a chance to prove that was not appealing.

The following week, however, I couldn't get rid of that frightening and unappealing thought. What would it look like if instead of asking God to help me be a nicer wife, I'd ask for opportunities today to treat Chris with love instead of sarcasm, patience instead of eye rolls, and joy instead of my often apathetic, expressionless, and irritated responses? How would my long-time prayer to be a gentler mom look differently if I prayed for opportunities today to act calmly instead of angrily when one of my teenagers inevitably ignores, overlooks, or is irritated by a request I give them?

What if instead of praying for humility, I asked for opportunities today to be okay with being wrong and failing to defend myself? Oh, my stomach…

The problem with praying for opportunities today is that it means I won't experience transformation from magical fairy dust, a painless lobotomy while I'm asleep, or other instantaneous methods. The problem with praying for opportunities today to look more like Christ is that it requires me to cooperate with God's answers to those prayers. Praying for opportunities today is hard and scary, and means I will have to do something. It also affords me the chance to practice becoming the person I wish I was and pray I'll become.

An area I struggle with daily is judgment. I love a lot of people in Jesus' name, but I don't usually like them very much. This week, when I had to be with someone I struggle with, I decided to pray the horrible thought. Instead of asking God to help me like them, I simply asked, as I was driving to be with them, that He would give me opportunities today to see the good in them. He provided those opportunities, and in that humbling moment, I realized that the more I pray for opportunities to look like Christ, little by little, the more I like the person I see looking back at me in the mirror.

• • • •

To Think About

As I was editing this piece for publication, I realized that I hadn't prayed specifically for an "opportunity today" for a very long time, possibly since shortly after I wrote this post. One of the reasons it's so imperative to continue reading God's Word daily is that God prompts our hearts and minds toward Him in a variety of ways. God uses pithy sayings, Christian friends, and even nature to help cement His Word in my heart. He is constantly helping me know His Word more deeply as I go about my day in fresh, new ways. I'm thankful that God helps me remember things by giving me short phrases and reminders, but I'm more thankful that He gives me them anew as I stay in and study His Word.

This week, will you pray for an opportunity each day to forgive, love, or be transformed? It is a difficult and courageous prayer, but also an effective one.

Disliking Your Husband's Wife

"Let us not become weary in doing good, for at the proper time we will reap a harvest if we do not give up."

Galatians 6:9

Week Twenty-Six

Today, I want to candidly share something I hope will help those of you who, like me, love your husband, but struggle to like his wife.

Although I love Jesus and speak and write about love, I can't seem to control my tone when I talk to my husband. Yes, I also struggle with how I talk to my kids (I just apologized to my daughter, Faithe, this morning for barking at her), but it's uglier and more consistent and pervasive toward Chris.

Since we've been married for twenty-five years and because Chris has shared with me how difficult and hurtful it is to be talked to in the condescending way I too often do to him, I'm grossly aware of my problem. I feel badly about it, pray about it literally daily, and apologize repeatedly.

But I can't seem to change.

Not long ago, we again had multiple moments of "intense fellowship," as my pastor calls marital disagreements, about my tone. As tired as Chris must get listening to me talk to him like he's 5 years old, I get tired of it being my default. I get tired of apologizing. I get tired of being the Jesus lady who can't seem to act very Jesus-y to the person I love most.

After our most recent argument and more prayer, God gave me a few epiphanies. First, I heard this Spirit-inspired question, "Would you ever talk to Kim like that?" Would I talk to my best friend, even if she was annoying me or doing something wrong, like I talk to Chris so easily and quickly? Shortly after having that thought, Chris said to me (unaware of my epiphany), "I just want you to talk to me like you talk to your friends." That's stuck with me.

The other Spirit-inspired thought was this. It's taken me forty-some years to get this way. I keep beating myself up for being unable to change, but God reminded me to give myself the grace and forgiveness He already has. He reminded me that regardless of how tired I am of being a jerk and apologizing for being a jerk, He loves me wildly. He reminded me when I most needed it that the moment I stop feeling loved or worthy of love and forgiveness is the moment I quit trying to be the wife I want to be.

The Author of love cares. He cares about the places we want to look differently but can't, and He cares about the people we hurt in the process. He cares by speaking to us when we want to give up. He cares by subtly whispering exactly what we need when we need it, and in doing so, reminds us that He loves us, even when we are struggling to like ourselves.

When we are continually reminded of His unconditional love, it becomes difficult to give up. If we quit, we will never change. But if we remain in His love, we can hold onto the hope that we will slowly, by the grace of God, begin to look more like Him.

. . . .

To Think About

I used to think my relationship with Christ depended on my loving Him, however, now I know that my relationship with Christ actually first depends on my understanding and experiencing His love for me. The order makes a major difference. When I thought I had to love Christ more in order to deepen my faith, know Him better, and act nicer, I was exhausted. But as I've been learning and internalizing the purpose and power of the cross, the more God's love has helped me deepen my faith, know Him better, and act nicer without trying quite as hard.

This week, keep asking God to show you His love. It is a bold prayer, but it's also a game changer.

Where's God?

"But he said to me, 'My grace is sufficient for you, my power is made perfect in weakness.'"

2 Corinthians 12:9a

Week Twenty-Seven

The last five weeks have been...exceptional. My son, who I'm incredibly close to, graduated high school and spent his first night on the campus he'll be attending in the fall. My oldest daughter shattered her finger at college. I was with her for what the doctor deemed "a complicated surgery" and helped her move (twice). Foley, the young man from the inner city we've been mentoring for the past five years, graduated from high school two weeks ago. We also had to make some difficult decisions with our international student who's called me Mom for two years. And, before my son's graduation party, I spoke at a memorial for a close friend who lost her husband.

Upon reflecting on all of this a few days ago, I felt that God had been distant. I began wondering where He'd been and why I hadn't felt a greater sense of His presence when I most needed Him. In doing so, I finally realized where I think He's been and what He's been doing.

I cry very easily, and I cry a lot. I've cried watching comedies like *Cheaper by the Dozen*, *Crazy Rich Asians*, and most Disney movies. I cry in crowds, small groups, and alone. I'm a crier. But in the past five weeks, I didn't cry at Foley or Casey's graduations. I didn't cry when Hannah had to have surgery, or while having hard conversations with our Chinese son, who I love. I didn't even cry speaking at the funeral.

Why?

Although I didn't cry at Casey's graduation, I cried on my prayer walk that morning and when Casey came into my room for his gown. He gave me a hug and kiss on the forehead, and when he turned to leave, I started sobbing, and I couldn't stop. I also didn't cry when Hannah got upset after finding out at the doctor that she had to have surgery the week of finals and moving, but when I got in the car after her appointment, I wept. I didn't cry while speaking at the funeral, but before I went up to share, there was a slide of my friend, her husband, and their daughters that not only made me cry, it literally took my breath away.

Where was God the past five weeks?

Holding me up.

I often wish I could feel God's arms around me or His peace wash over me in a palpable way, but I now know that I didn't need a hug or a bath. I needed His strength.

My son and Foley were ecstatic to be graduating and needed to know I was ecstatic for them. My daughter needed me to remind her everything would work out. My friend wanted me to share with those attending the funeral the Reason she's traversing the loss of her husband with courage and peace. Everyone I love and who my heart has broken for over the past five weeks needed me to be okay. God, in His grace, allowed me to be just that when I most needed it. But He also gave me space to lose it when no one was looking.

Where's God when we need Him? The same place He is when we think we don't.

Close to our hearts.

· · · ·

To Think About

Paul says in 2 Corinthians 12 that when we are weak, Christ's strength is made perfect in us. I have always wondered how that passage manifests itself in everyday life. I've often prayed and asked God for His strength the morning after I was up all night with a sick child or when I felt nervous and unequipped before teaching. I suppose I want and expect Christ's strength to give me superpowers. I want obvious, palpable, and practical help, but usually, like many other things in our faith walk, although God is subtle and seems slow, He personally, intimately, and lovingly provides only and exactly all we need.

This week, keep asking for Christ's strength in your weakness!

Swamp Flowers

"Remain in me, and I will remain in you.
No branch can bear fruit by itself; it must
remain in the vine. Neither can you bear
fruit unless you remain in me."

John 15:4

Week Twenty-Eight

My homework assignment for my discipleship group last week was to spend time enjoying God. I know how to read my Bible and pray, but enjoying God is a completely confusing and unfamiliar exercise for me.

I tried enjoying God by listening to worship music while driving, but it reminded me of algebra. I didn't get it. The part of my brain that does math and enjoys God must be broken. I tried a few other times in different ways to enjoy God, but those attempts were always stressful and contrived.

A few weeks ago, I got to my dentist early, and his office is along a riverwalk, so I thought I'd try enjoying God again. Just when I was feeling totally guilty for wasting time on a walk, a woman walking past me on the trail asked if I'd seen the marsh marigolds. I hadn't and didn't really care, but she was so exuberant that I wondered if I should go after my appointment and find them. Maybe my hallelujah moment of enjoying God would happen in the field of beautiful flowers.

After the appointment, on my way to find said flowers, I was again bored and confused. I passed a couple on the path and thought maybe I should imagine Jesus walking beside me. I laughed at how weird that was, then took a selfie of me and Jesus (to amuse myself). When I was about to give up trying to enjoy Jesus, I had an unusual thought. I realized that if Jesus was walking beside me, I'd be totally invincible. I'd be safe and protected. And, for whatever reason, that thought made me teary.

But I had a luscious, amazing field of flowers to find, so I kept walking.

When I got to where the beautiful flowers were supposed to be, I saw nothing. What a rip-off. I headed back to my car annoyed and frustrated. About halfway back, however, something caught my eye. Marsh marigolds. All three of them. Really? What a waste.

When I got home and reflected on everything, I realized that enjoying God was exactly like my hunt for flowers. I wanted enjoying God to be overwhelming and obvious. But just like I sailed past the swamp flowers the woman was amazed by, I sailed past God giving me a sense of His constant protection and presence because I wanted something more glamorous.

When I was recently waiting for a loved one during a two-hour surgery and feeling alone and afraid, I remembered my walk with Jesus. I remembered feeling safe and protected because Jesus was beside me. Suddenly, I realized that Jesus was also beside me in that OR.

What did I learn about enjoying God? The disciplines of faith we don't feel like doing or understand aren't for God. They're for us. When we persevere in them, they protect us and remind us of His loving presence. And no matter how hard finding God may seem at times, once He's really walked beside you and you've sensed His presence, His beauty is completely and utterly breathtaking.

• • • •

To Think About

What makes it difficult for you to persevere in the disciplines of the faith? Have you stopped reading your Bible daily because you find it confusing, boring, or impractical? Do you pray the same monotonous prayers at dinner and bedtime because you aren't sure God hears your prayers? Have you stopped spending time with God (or never started) because your to-do list edges Him out?

I once felt convicted about praying more specifically for each of my kids, but realistically, I didn't know where I was going to make time daily to do that. I prayed and asked God for help. I eventually got the Spirit-inspired idea to pray on Mondays more earnestly for my youngest child, Tuesdays for my son, Wednesdays for my oldest child, and Thursdays for my husband.

Obviously, spiritual disciplines don't save us. We are saved by grace, through faith, but as Dallas Willard said, "Grace is not opposed to effort, it is opposed to earning. Earning is an attitude. Effort is an action."

This week, talk honestly to God about your questions and struggles with reading the Bible or with being in prayer or Christian community. As you pray, remember that the disciplines of the faith are meant to help you experience Christ's love more deeply and consistently.

Back to Normal

"...give thanks in all circumstances; for this is God's will for you in Christ Jesus."

1 Thessalonians 5:18

Week Twenty-Nine

Three weeks ago, my dad suffered a heart attack.

Everything changed that day. I realized how much I adore my parents. I found real strength in and through Christ in my hardest, most exhausting and emotional days in the ICU. I saw the legitimate and undeniable power that comes when people pray. I became grateful for things I took for granted every day: an appetite, the ability to smile, and life.

But within a week of my dad being taken to the hospital in a helicopter and not knowing for three hours if he was even alive, not only was life back to normal, I was back to normal.

I was back to life after being gone for eight days, back to speaking engagements, grad school, and Thanksgiving. Back to being busy, ungrateful, and taking life for granted. Within just a few weeks, I went from being thankful for the sun shining to being constantly anxious, edgy, and filled with complaints.

Yesterday was no exception. I didn't have time. I didn't have time to drive to Hope Street, the transitional living facility in the inner city where I volunteer. I didn't have time to attend the weekly prayer meeting or interview members there for my grad class, and when I think I don't have time to do something, my mood is exceptionally foul. As I drove to Hope Street filled with consternation, I drove past a man living out of two trash bags and a wire cart, and I felt nothing but selfish, justified angst.

When I arrived for prayer, I apologized for being late and

sat quietly, faking a smile, until George walked in. I'd never met George before, but when you live at Hope Street, it's usually because you aren't able to live somewhere else. The people at Hope Street were formerly addicted, homeless, incarcerated, or in some other place of brokenness.

George was my age, but sat down very slowly. He grimaced and held the arms of the chair he was getting into very tightly. When a staff member asked George how he was, he said, again very slowly, "Wonderful." He went on, "In fact, I'd have to think long and hard for something to complain about."

God answers my prayers in the most unpredictable ways. The Lord knew I could barely stand being around myself lately. He knew I was tired of listening to myself complain but couldn't seem to stop. He knew I was grateful deep down for so many big things but had forgotten to be thankful for the small things. He also knew I wouldn't be able to hear from him until I was forced to sit long enough to listen.

And because He loves me the same whether I'm helping my dad or angrily driving to a prayer meeting, He answered my prayer in the most gentle, kind, and meaningful way—through a broken and humble man named George who came late to a prayer meeting to remind me how joyful, free, and content gratitude looks.

• • • •

To Think About

I've known for many years that my default is to complain. I go quickly and easily to negative spaces, worst-case scenarios, and feeling sorry for myself. Since realizing that about myself, I've wanted to change, but I've wanted that change to happen in one grandiose epiphany and I've wanted it to be permanent. Unfortunately, back in reality, transformation generally happens gradually and is manifested through boring and almost imperceptible opportunities presented to me in everyday life. Do you want to be more grateful and positive?

This week, look around at the people and situations right in front of you and thank God for them. If you are struggling, like I was, to even bring yourself to do that, then be honest and tell God that. Thankfully, the Lord meets us where we really are and adds to our faith in "increasing measure" (2 Peter 1:5-9).

Reaching the End of My Rope

"...but pity anyone who falls and has no one to help them up."

Ecclesiastes 4:10b

Week Thirty

A few months ago, I had a meltdown. I literally wanted to throw my laptop like a frisbee out the nearest window or run it over with my car. I had been working on a piece to submit to a magazine that I'd written for a few times before, and I couldn't. It wouldn't. I didn't.

I was frustrated and ready to give up, so I called Shelly.

I asked my friend, who is an author and editor, to meet for coffee. I told her about my rage writing, and she understood. She had been there and could relate to my anguish.

I think we empathize well when we've been there. I once heard a pastor teach about empathy. He was a marathon runner who ran the same route almost every day while training for a race. One day, he kept passing the same runner on the track. At first, they nodded at each other. The second time around, they smiled. On the third lap, they gave each other a thumbs-up. Around the tenth lap, the other runner stopped dead in his tracks. He looked at the pastor and started swinging his arm around like a windmill, shouting with exuberance, "You go, you go, you go!!!" That energy, passion, and encouragement was exactly what the pastor needed to train hard and finish well.

Conversely, several months later, around the 20-mile mark of the LA marathon, the pastor passed a group of coffee-toting, donut-eating, chair-dwelling spectators. With the best of intentions, they started cheering and said, "You've got this! You're almost to the end!" The pastor said he felt like slapping their donuts and coffee out of their hands as he ran by. Encouragement from spectators who have never run further than their local bakery, even if well-intended, isn't as meaningful or helpful as it is from those running the race alongside us.

Shelly has wanted to throw her computer out the window before. She has worked for hours on a piece only to hit "save" and never look at it again. She has felt the regret of wasted time and coming up with absolutely nothing despite her best efforts.

So what advice did Shelly give me? She said that writing is hard, but that time spent writing is never wasted. She told me that I was a gifted writer and not to give up. After that, she sent me emails weekly, encouraging me.

There are countless stories in the Bible about friends like Shelly. Friends who held their friends up when they were weak (Exodus 17:11-12), who were loyal and dependable (1 Samuel 20), and who encouraged others (Deuteronomy 31:7-8). Despite the fact that the Christian life was never meant to be walked alone, so often, in the name of efficiency, pride, or embarrassment, we go it alone until we fail, fall, or both. However, that was never God's design for humankind.

I am currently working on the most difficult writing project I've ever attempted. I have written, rewritten, edited, and reedited for hours. I have wanted to give up. I have loved parts of what I've written and hated others. But in the end, I'm not giving up. I have this voice that tells me that the purpose for which I am writing is greater than me. I know that good or bad, successful or not, I must keep competing because, in the end, I will have gotten off my chair and raced. Thank you, Shelly.

••••

To Think About

Do you have a Shelly in your life to encourage you in a struggle? Are you being a Shelly to someone else who needs genuine encouragement? If you answered no to either of those questions, take a minute this week to ask the Lord if He wants you to change that. He never intended us to follow Him alone, but in the strength, wisdom, and encouragement of community.

If you do have a Shelly, take time this week to thank God for that person, and maybe write them a note thanking them for being your sister in Christ.

Bone Scans and Biopsies

"The thief comes only to steal and kill and destroy; I have come that they may have life, and have it to the full."

John 10:10

Week Thirty-One

Although God has freed me from many of my fears over time, my lifelong battle with panic attacks and anxiety is still a struggle. Over the last several weeks, however, by God's grace, I've noticed something about the evolution of worry in my life.

Recently, the dermatologist told my husband that a spot on his hand "looked cancerous." He had a sample taken for the biopsy, and we waited. After two years of trying to diagnose the cause of a nagging pain in my ribs, my doctor convinced me that I should have a bone scan to rule out cancer. I scheduled the scan and waited.

For some, waiting isn't a big deal. I know. I'm married to someone with very low blood pressure. Very low. He rarely worries about anything. Ever. People like me, however, always imagine the worst scenario. I don't have an earache, I have a tumor. It's not a rash, it's shingles (which it actually was once). This time, however, when I heard cancer (twice), something unprecedented happened.

The three weeks of waiting for my husband's biopsy and my bone scan results were...different. I was present with my family instead of being preoccupied with "what-ifs." I enjoyed every day without that gnawing pit of anxiety in my stomach. I was rational and reasonable instead of wasting time searching Google for a diagnosis. Although the relaxed among us can't appreciate what a big deal this is, those of you who live too often with a spirit of fear can. How can I explain my peace-filled waiting?

For five years, I've asked God to show me His love in a tangible, undeniable, real way. Part of the reason for that request was a verse in 1 John that I never understood: "There is no fear in love..." Although God had liberated me from so much anxiety over the years, I always wondered why I was still so fearful when I loved God so much. After five years of learning, waiting, and praying, I'm finally beginning to understand why I still struggle with fear, despite how much I love God.

I never understood 1 John 4:18 because I thought being less fearful was contingent on my love for God. Rather than focusing on God's unconditional and perfect love for me, I was always trying to love God "more" by being better and trying harder. I never experienced more lasting peace because I did with that verse what I do with a lot of things.

I made it about me.

However, the more I experience God's love in my heart, not just acknowledge it in my mind, I'm finding I'm calmer. The more I feel and know deeply that Christ's unconditional, radical, unchanging love has nothing to do with what I do or don't do, the more naturally and readily I'm trusting Him. And when in less than three weeks, you're waiting for multiple test results without fear, you can't help but feel deeply loved.

P.S. All test results were negative.

• • • •

To Think About

Do you think more about showing God how much you love Him through your words and actions, or are you more concerned about knowing and experiencing His love more and more? One way I realized I was more concerned about trying to love God than know His love was by looking in my Bible. Most of the things I underlined and highlighted were about what I should or shouldn't do: "...in your anger, do not sin." "Do not let any unwholesome talk come out of your mouth." "Honor your father and mother." Honoring God in your words and actions is important, but I'm learning that the more concerned I am with experiencing and knowing God's love for me, the easier it is to look more like Christ with less effort.

This week, try reading your Bible not to find out what you should do, but instead to find out more about who God is and how much He loves you. It's easy to believe that God loves your best friend, your daughter, or your pastor. Believing and accepting the fact that God loves you is harder and takes more time, but it's how we move closer to a life of freedom and change.

How to Love People Who Are Hard to Like

"Love is patient and kind; love does not envy or boast; it is not arrogant or rude. It does not insist on its own way; it is not irritable or resentful; it does not rejoice at wrongdoing, but rejoices with the truth. Love bears all things, believes all things, hopes all things, endures all things."

1 Corinthians 13:4-7 (ESV)

Week Thirty-Two

When our Chinese student, Zu, had been with us for only a short time, we realized that he was...different. Unlike the Chinese student who lived with us last year or his Chinese peers at school, Zu is more into being social and popular than studying. He struggles to listen, follow rules, and wake up on time. After my dad's heart attack, I wasn't sure I was going to have the time (or patience) needed to parent Zu well. I eventually decided to start praying four words, every morning:

Help me love Zu.

I already liked Zu. He's funny, polite, and endearing. He likes my cooking, puts his dishes in the dishwasher, and loves worship music. But when he'd talk back or was on his phone instead of doing homework (after I'd just told him to get off his phone and do his homework), my love-o-meter malfunctioned. I became increasingly irritated by any little thing he did or failed to do that wasn't remotely...perfect.

At a recent wrestling match, Zu's opponent was ginormous. I was sick from nervousness, but then had a thought. I'm sure it wasn't one of those "Spirit-inspired" thoughts I often talk about because the violence of it surprised even me: "If that boy hurts Zu, I'll hurt him." I'm not sure how a slightly out-of-shape, middle-aged woman could so much as lay a finger on a teenage wrestler who resembled the Hulk, but I had apparently lost all rational thinking at this point.

When we got home from wrestling, Zu was frantically trying to do laundry. It was late, and another load was going, so I told Zu that I'd do it. When you're in high school at our house, Mom doesn't do your laundry (strike one). The next morning, Zu overslept (again), so I ran down and woke him up. When you're in high school at our house, Mom doesn't wake you up (strike two). Then, before strike three, I realized something. I wasn't mad or frustrated about the laundry or him oversleeping. I realized that my only threatening thoughts regarding Zu recently had been directed toward Hulk boy. And that's when I realized...

I love Zu.

Two months ago, I would've loved Zu too...if he would've been "better." If he would've studied and listened. Today, I realized that Zu still isn't into homework, his room is still messy, and I'm certain his phone has actually morphed into an appendage. So what changed? The same thing that recently changed for me in understanding God's love.

Timothy Keller says that we hope our performance leads to a verdict, that our good behavior will help us go to heaven and earn God's approval. But at the cross, Christ already gave the verdict: we are loved and forgiven.[7]

That verdict now leads us to perform, but not the other way around.

I believe that, but don't. I know that, but forget. I want to love like Christ loves me, but I need to ask God for help.

And in His reverse economy, when I ask for help, He changes my heart and fills it to overflowing.

••••

[7] Keller, Timothy. *The Freedom of Self-Forgetfulness: The Path to True Christian Joy*, 37-44. Leyland, England: 10Publishing, 2017.

To Think About

Who is difficult to love in your life right now? Perhaps you can't imagine a world where you like that person, let alone love them. Regardless of how justified you may feel in your disdain toward that person, because of the Holy Spirit in us, we are conflicted in our souls when we fail to love. We think repeatedly about the person, how we were wronged, and what we did right in the relationship. I'm learning with a difficult relationship I'm in right now that when I am not at peace in my soul about someone, I'm not in the center of God's will. I'm praying every day that God will help me love this person and, regardless of whether or not there is resolution in the relationship, that He will help me be at peace in my heart toward this individual.

Perhaps you want to pray the same thing this week for someone who is difficult to love. And remember, peace doesn't just bring glory to God. It is a gift to us as well!

You Prayed Once?

"...your kingdom come, your will be done, on earth as it is in heaven."

Matthew 6:10

Week Thirty-Three

The other day, I went to Bible study with my BFF, and I cried, complained, verbally vomited on her, and swore once or twice.

The end.

Why would I share my deeply profound and moving time in God's Word with you?

The day before my tirade, I read a post from a young blogger who decided one night that she was done trying to find a boyfriend. She knew God's timing and boyfriend-finding skills were better than hers, so she decided to leave it up to God.

The very next day, God brought her the man of her dreams.

Although the romantic in me liked this story, the part of me that lives on planet earth didn't. I like the young woman's faith. I like how she stopped relying on herself and went to God. I fully believe God brought her a godly and wonderful man the day after she prayed about it. However, I struggle with the immediacy, ease, and neatness of it (mostly because of my own ugly, frustrating, and disappointing week of being a Christian).

Why would I tell you about my time in God's Word cloaked with profanity and proverbial puke?

Although sometimes we pray for things once and the next day get what we prayed for, that sometimes is rare. My walk with Christ, and I believe most people's walk with Christ, is beautiful, awful, messy, arduous, confusing, amazing, sometimes filled with hope, and other times with our own hypocrisy. Just when

I see God grow me, in His love He reveals something ugly in me that, although He's already forgiven me, He wants to free me from. As many days as I'm inspired and transformed, there are more days that I'm annoyed and frustrated.

If you prayed for something last night and it came true today, I truly am so happy for you (kind of). But if you're like me and you're tired of being a disappointment to yourself, I'm so grateful for your company. If you're like me and had more of a throw-up-on-your-friend kind of day than met-your-dream-man kind of day, know that is what most of my time as a Christ-follower has looked like.

Why would I tell you how depressing my Bible study was this morning?

Because being a Christian isn't about finding Mr. Right, answered prayer, and perfect people. Being a Christian means being human, and being human is not pretty. Being a Christian means praying the same thing over and over again, sometimes without ever getting what you asked for. Being a Christian means expecting more difficulty than delight, but trusting either way that there still isn't anything, anyone, or any answer better than Christ.

· · · ·

To Think About

When you pray, do you ask and genuinely desire God's will to be done? Or are you like me and pray with your own agenda, hopes, and desired outcomes? I think most people pray like I do, however, I am beginning to move toward trying to surrender the outcome of my prayers to the Lord. Moving to a place where we start to trust God with our prayer requests takes a lot of time, honesty, and frequent surrender.

If you haven't ever prayed for God's will to be done, this week ask Him for help in doing so. He always meets us where we are, but also loves us too much to leave us there.

Why Peter's My Favorite

"The most important requirement of prayer is firmly holding on to God and believing that he is merciful and compassionate— someone who wants to help us."

Martin Luther

Week Thirty-Four

A few weeks ago, I wrote about my struggle, not with the fact that I get mad, use sarcasm, and generally wish most things I say wouldn't come out of my mouth, but that all of those things, and more, are my default. I lamented that my husband, who doesn't try as hard as I do, read his Bible daily, or teach it to others professionally, defaults to kindness, selflessness, and patience. I have since told him that I have considered marrying someone else less perfect, however, I do not think that's the solution.

I have spent a great amount of time praying and thinking about why I don't look and act differently. Why, despite intentional prayer, effort, and even giving up and waiting for God to help, these things do not seem to help me avoid being an almost constant disappointment to myself. What have I concluded about being the way I am?

Personalities are Different. My husband helps with math homework, and I help with English. He loves problem-solving, and I love taking pictures. Chris loves cooking, and I love eating. Although my mouth can be a problem, it is also sometimes an encouragement. I am passionate and emotional, which sometimes leads to road rage, but it also sometimes leads to things like mentoring our inner-city orphan. My husband reminded me that some of what I struggle with is merely that we are wired differently. I am trying to work on looking at more of the positive sides of mine while gracefully working on the negative.

I Don't Blame My Kids. One morning, while praying about why I'm a hot mess, I thought about two of my kids. One of my kids is a lot like their dad: mild-mannered, not easily offended, and accepts constructive criticism well. Another one of my kids is more like me (the opposite of the former list). They are two years apart in age, share the same gene pool, and were raised very similarly. I would never think child B has an innate character flaw. I would not hold child A above child B because they are wired differently. God often uses the view I have of my children to remind me how He sees me. I am trying to remember that as I pray about places I want to look and act differently.

Peter's Always Been My Favorite. I have always been partial to Peter in the Bible. He always said what everyone else was thinking but were too discerning or cowardly to say. He often got things wrong, was scolded by Jesus, and made mistakes. Peter betrayed Jesus three times, and although Jesus knew fully well that he was going to do that, Jesus still suffered and died for him.

My husband once said to me that part of transforming is becoming aware. Although I apologize to him a lot, a few years ago, I wouldn't have realized or probably have cared that much that I hurt him. Part of transforming continues to be depending on the One who knew I was going to default to words, thoughts, and actions I didn't want to, which is why He had to go to the cross at all. That's love. Love worth trying to continue to imitate. Love worth persevering for the rest of my life.

• • • •

To Think About

What is an area of default for you that you loathe? Being late, losing your cool, or blaming others? How do you talk to yourself when you default to your default? Although I feel justified in the moment, when I later realize I did (fill-in-the-blank) again, I always used to beat myself up relentlessly. The Bible says in Romans 8:1, however, that there is no condemnation for those who are in Christ Jesus.

This week, when you default to hostility, violence, or profanity, allow God's conviction to love you into transformation, but don't beat yourself up.

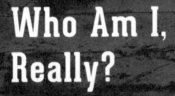

Who Am I, Really?

"Therefore, if anyone is in Christ, he is a new creation. The old has gone, the new has come!"

2 Corinthians 5:17

Week Thirty-Five

I've been learning many things recently about identity. Not what I say my identity is grounded in, but the identity I respond to and live out of. Although I thought my identity was grounded in being a daughter of the King, it isn't.

One of the ways we can discover the identity we are grounded in is by paying close attention to the emotions people evoke in us. Over the last several months, I've noticed that I often respond to others with anger and defensiveness. I've learned that I don't live out my identity in Christ, but I live out the false belief that I'm not good enough, smart enough, talented enough, pretty enough, and seven or eight other not-enoughs. (Or maybe twelve. Or eighteen.)

After realizing this over the course of several weeks, I've been asking God to help me trust what He says about me. I've been asking Him to help me trust that His perfect love and acceptance are enough. I'm asking God to help me live out my identity as being good enough by His standards, regardless of what I or anyone else thinks of me.

It's humbling to realize that I function out of a middle school perception of myself and that it's the root of some of my defensiveness, anger, and hypersensitivity. However, I was excited to watch God help me begin grounding my identity in Him. It's exhausting being a people-pleaser. It's hard work biting my husband's head off when he simply asks a question or makes a suggestion. I was tired of spending so much mental time and energy ensuring I looked my best. So, I've been asking God to help me trust His perfect love and acceptance, and it has been freeing and amazing.

Until now.

The more I've been asking God to help me trust that His perfect love and acceptance are enough, the more He has also shown me that He perfectly loves and accepts everyone around me. As He shows me His deep love and acceptance for me, regardless of how smart I am or how I look, He's also been reminding me that He deeply loves my know-it-all friend, that condescending woman I can't stand, and people who drive slow in the fast lane.

Brennan Manning says in *The Ragamuffin Gospel*, "How I treat a brother or sister from day to day, how I react to the sin-scarred wino on the street, how I respond to interruptions from people I dislike, how I deal with normal people in their normal confusion on a normal day may be a better indication of my reverence for life than the anti-abortion sticker on the bumper of my car."[8]

As I learn to trust Christ's perfect, unconditional love and acceptance for me regardless of whether or not I feel I'm enough, God is helping me remember that because everyone else is perfectly loved and accepted by Him too, I have no excuse. He's teaching me that I have many double standards. He's teaching me that because of His extravagant love for me, when I can love "normal people in their normal confusion on a normal day," I will know I have started to identify and live out of His perfect love and acceptance for me.

• • • •

[8] Manning, Brennan. *The Ragamuffin Gospel*, 141. Colorado Springs, CO: Multnomah Books, 2005.

To Think About

Think of a person who bothers you. Maybe they're condescending, arrogant, or perhaps they seem to ignore you. Something that has been helping me continue to assess whether my identity is steeped in Christ or in the opinions and actions of others is by replacing the word "others" in Philippians 2:3 with the name of someone I struggle to like:

"Do nothing out of selfish ambition or vain conceit. But in humility consider (insert your co-worker, in-law, or friend's name here) better than yourselves."

This is a difficult exercise, but this week, let's pray, think, and wrestle through what makes this hard and the fact that Christ humbled Himself to the cross for (insert your name).

Dear Four-Years-Ago Self

"So give your servant a discerning heart to govern your people and to distinguish between right and wrong. For who is able to govern this great people of yours?"

1 Kings 3:9

Week Thirty-Six

Dear Four-Years-Ago Self,

Everyone's telling you that now that your child's in high school, it's going to go fast. They say, "Don't blink or you'll miss it." You already know and are dreading how quickly high school is going to go, but what can you do about it, right?

A lot.

Be Present. The infrequent times the kids are home, put down your to-do list, put down your phone, and quit cleaning. The dirt isn't going anywhere, so clean enough to function. Get off social media and be available. Sometimes they'll talk to you or give you a hug, but often they'll ignore your existence and you'll think it doesn't matter if you're there or not.

It matters.

Remember. Even though you'll try to do everything right and balance lectures and love, they're going to dislike you sometimes. (If they like you all the time, you're not being a parent, which is what they need. You're being a friend, which they probably already have in abundance.) They may answer you with grunts and eye rolls. So, ask God to help you remember when you were 16. Ask Him to remind you of those hard years of peer pressure and having, then breaking up with, that first crush. Being a teenager seems easy when you're 40, but when God has let me remember teenager me,

I've parented with less regret.

Kneel. Years ago, when parents would tell me that their secret to raising teenagers was prayer, I smiled and longed for a practical, replicable answer. Now I know prayer is that answer and thank God. Prayer is a treasure, and it's mostly for you. When you pray the first time they drive alone, go on their first date, or take their ACT, it will change, challenge, and protect you. What you believe about God, faith, and prayer will never be challenged more than it will over the next four years, and

Thank God.

Expect Mistakes. You're going to try to ensure they don't do what you did in high school. You're going to parent based on what they can become or what you're afraid they won't. You're going to want to protect them from struggling, failing, and hurting. That's normal, but unrealistic. So, when they do mess up, pray and ask the Lord for wisdom. Don't dread inevitable mistakes,

Use them.

Don't Forget You. It will not be pretty, healthy, or beneficial for you to be a broken, needy mess when they leave the house. (And they will leave, which is good for them and you, though it will feel very not good). So, start thinking about your next season now. Date your husband again. Remember what you enjoyed before kids. Learn that thing you always wished you would've. You need a life, and they'll want to know you have one when they leave.

The Lord is gracious, Four-Years-Ago Self. Try not to dread the end of the next four years, but enjoy every moment, in the moment. Give yourself and them plenty of grace. The four years will go quickly, but when they end, you're still Mom.

And that will never change.

. . . .

To Think About

Whether you are a mom or not, saying goodbye to loved ones, relationships, and seasons is difficult. One of the things that has gotten me through goodbyes is trying to focus on what I can be thankful for.

What can you praise God for this week? Don't turn the page or close the book before you actually do just that, and then do it again tomorrow.

Road Rage On My Way to Church

"The Bible's purpose is not so much to show you how to live a good life. The Bible's purpose is to show you how God's grace breaks into your life against your will and saves you from the sin and brokenness, otherwise you would never be able to overcome...religion is 'if you obey, then you will be accepted.' But the Gospel is, 'if you are absolutely accepted, and sure you're accepted, only then will you ever begin to obey'. Those are two utterly different things. Every page of the Bible shows the difference."

Timothy Keller

Week Thirty-Seven

Not long ago, I had an encounter with a boy I didn't realize was autistic. I wrote a blog post afterwards about being convicted that I shouldn't be more patient, loving, and kind just because someone has special needs. We all have special needs. We all have a back story, struggles, and hurts.

I loved that epiphany. I appreciated God reminding me that I need to slow down, take time, and give grace to everyone. Although it's embarrassing to realize that I have different standards and levels of patience and tolerance for "normal people," I was grateful for the revelation and challenge of trying to see everyone as God does: special, deserving of love, and worthy of time and attention.

But that was then.

The next morning, I left for my discipleship group as I always do. Late. I raced out the door angry and frustrated, wondering why I was always late and could never seem to leave in a calm, organized, and on-time fashion. But when I'm late, I don't take ownership. I plow people over who are "in my way" and blame them for my perpetual tardiness.

On my way to church, a truck on the freeway started tailgating me. I couldn't go any faster because of the car in front of me, and I couldn't get into another lane. So, I decided to let Truck Guy know he was following too closely and tapped my brakes. He didn't like that and got closer, so I did it again. Once

I could change lanes to let Truck Guy pass, we mouthed hostile words and gave angry glances to each other. I finally arrived at church (no, the irony is not lost on me) and tried forgetting my morning.

Afterwards, however, I began feeling remorseful. Remorseful that I left the house angry and irritated, again. Remorseful (kind of) that I was filled with such angst toward Truck Guy. Remorseful that I can passionately desire to love others one day and the next I'm trying to run them off the road.

After praying, reading Scripture, and lamenting about this for a while, God reminded me of some things. He reminded me that Christ doesn't love me more when I write a post about an autistic boy than He does when I swear at people, and He challenged whether I really believed that. He reminded me how beautiful and broken we are and how we can love then loath almost simultaneously. He reminded me that I can be helpful and hateful in a single day. In a single hour. In five minutes.

But His grace covers it all.

The more deeply we mess up, the more grace means to us. The more repeatedly we fail, the more grateful we are for forgiveness. The more grace we've been given, the harder it becomes to justify failing to extend it to others, repeatedly...

Every day. Every hour. Every five minutes.

• • • •

To Think About

While my kids were young, I was habitually my ugliest when trying to get to church, yet once we arrived, I would put on a sane, happy face. When I would get into worship, however, I felt like a poser. I wondered what my children would someday tell their therapists about my hypocrisy and lunacy. It was in those moments where I began to realize that I didn't really believe in the core of my heart that I was fully known and fully loved and delighted in by God.

This week, when you have your ugly on, think about how God sees you. Question whether or not you think He loves you just as much in your sin as He does when you're feeling sanctified.

Struggling
to Love

"If any one of you is without
sin, let him be the first to
throw a stone at her."

John 8:7b

Week Thirty-Eight

A few weeks ago, I attended a workshop that taught church leaders how to love the LGBT community. I was reminded that when I avoid and condemn LGBT folks, I have no chance of sharing Christ's love with them. I was reminded that I do not need to approve of the choices of a person who identifies as LGBT in order to love them (I don't approve of my own choices half the time), and I learned that though some believe it's contradictory to the gospel to love LGBT folks, showing them love and acceptance actually fulfills it. Although I knew most of this, agreed with it, and want to love the gay community, there's a problem.

When I watched a male commentator during the last Olympics wearing nicer women's clothing than me (and looking better than me) or when I encounter a loud male barista talking extremely effeminately, I'm uncomfortable. I'm not around many LGBT folks, don't have many gay friends or family members, and it's not something I grew up with. I know some people reading this will stop here because you don't like my honesty.

But when we fail to be honest, we fail to relate, learn, and grow.

When I was getting my education degree and encountered gated parking lots, barred windows, and patrolled elementary schools where I taught in the inner city, I was also uncomfortable. I grew up in northern Wisconsin with nine hundred white people (except me, my mom, and brothers). I wasn't uncomfortable teaching in the city because I was racist. I was uncomfortable because I was sheltered (and still am).

Being uncomfortable isn't the problem. Staying there is.

So, I've been asking God once again to help me love. Despite our best intentions, desires, and hopes, we are human. I know I should love everyone, but I don't. Heck, I can't even love people who are too nice and happy or smile excessively. I also know that Christ knows my heart. He knows that I want to love people who are different from me or who I just don't understand. So, I'm asking God to help me love LGBT folks, loud or quiet, flamboyant or subtle.

While vacationing in Arizona recently, God answered me. I saw several gay couples, baristas, and families while out eating, hiking, and sightseeing, but this time I noticed moms instead of mannerisms. I saw couples instead of choices. In seeing our common humanity, I suddenly became more comfortable. When, without even thinking about it, I asked a gay couple in the Grand Canyon if I could take their picture for them (it's hard taking a selfie with that expansive beauty in the background), I knew God was helping me love.

Who do you want to love? Your in-laws, coworker, or a gay neighbor? Whenever God answers my prayers to help me love others (and He always does, though often slowly), I ironically find it easier to love someone else He wants me to love more like He does too.

Myself.

· · · ·

To Think About

I mentioned above that, "I learned that though some believe it's contradictory to the gospel to love LGBT folks, showing them love and acceptance actually fulfills it." Do you agree or disagree with this statement? What Biblical evidence can you cite to support your position?

This week, spend time praying about the Biblical evidence you find and the struggles you may have loving people who identify as LGBT.

How to Love Difficult People

"When He tells us to love our enemies, He gives, along with the command, the love itself."

Corrie ten Boom[9]

Week Thirty-Nine

When I came home from a visit to China recently, I wrote about my desire to worry less and to live and love better as I had done almost instinctively while traveling. I came back desiring to look more like I did in Asia because the reality is that I can slip back into complacency, anxiety, and lovelessness quickly and imperceptibly. Did praying help?

Unfortunately, yes.

I was recently lamenting to someone about our international student. He was a challenge for us when he first came to live with us, but eventually, I began to see my prayers to love him answered subtly and unconventionally. Unfortunately, toward the end of the school year, Zu reverted to some old behaviors. When I was complaining to my friend about this, they asked why we were having him back this year. The question rocked me.

Why have we hosted international students for ten months out of the year for the last two years? I like my privacy. I like spending time with just my family on the rare occasions that actually happens. I like one less thing to do, not one more. Why were we having Zu back when it's inconvenient and I often complain about him?

I wanted the answer to be to share Christ's love. Although that's partly true, the bigger reason is that I feel bad. I feel bad that these students are thousands of miles from home, and if we don't host them, they'll live in apartments with other Chinese

9 ten Boom, Corrie. *The Hiding Place*, 248. Grand Rapids, MI: Bantam Books, 1984.

students. They probably eat cereal and Pop-Tarts for dinner, and no one will hug, nurture, or love them. That bothers me, so we have, reluctantly at times, opened our home.

When I thought about all of this, I realized that Zu had nothing to do with my lament. He did not ask to stay with us last year. He knew nothing about us. No one forced us to host him.

When I thought even more about all of this, I also realized that I haven't loved Zu.

God, in His grace, brought me a long way in tolerating, liking, and trying to love Zu last year; however, I had not loved him like I loved my kids or the way I would want someone to love them. I loved him when he deserved it and it didn't inconvenience me. I loved him conditionally. But conditional love isn't really love at all.

Has prayer helped me love better? Yes, but not in the warm, fuzzy way I'd hoped. I'm learning to love by having the dark, ugly places in my heart exposed. Not only had I failed to love Zu well, I believed I had.

Jeremiah 17:9 says, "The heart is deceitful above all things." It's easy for me to see duplicity in others yet totally miss my own hypocrisy. I often ask God for romantic things I think I want, hoping the answer will come in a pretty package with a bow. I hope the answer to my prayers will happen to me, rather than the solution involving and including me. God knows, however, that I genuinely want to change, grow, and love better. In His love, His answers are simple. In His love, God's response to my requests often come in the form of the opportunity to merely love the people right in front of me, *deeply and authentically.*

• • • •

[10] Chambers, Oswald. *My Utmost for His Highest*, May 11th devotional. Uhrichsville, OH: Barbour Books, 1963.

To Think About

Is there someone in your life you have to try hard to love (or even like)? Oswald Chambers said, "God's love to me is inexhaustible, and I must love others from the bedrock of God's love to me."[10] Recently, someone I love hurt my feelings, multiple times. I'm struggling, to say the least, to love and forgive them, but in that, I'm relearning that trying harder or rationalizing why I should love or forgive them doesn't work. In order for me to love and forgive in my heart, I've been praying and asking God to help me know and be reminded of His love and forgiveness toward me. Slowly, as I continue to wait and pray, He whispers to me through His Word and His Spirit. Slowly, I am beginning to experience more of His love, grace, and personal concern for me, and in that, I am softening. In that, He is deconstructing my hurt, pride, and what I feel I am owed. In that, His love is becoming a deeper, larger, and more solid bedrock for me.

This week, don't ask God to help you love someone without first asking Him to remind you of His love for you. The order matters!

Lessons Along the Wait

"I say to myself, 'The LORD is my portion; therefore I will wait for him.'"

Lamentations 3:24

Week Forty

My son recently asked me a question I've asked myself a million times. "Why do you have to be so angry?" I was irritated he had put his dirty dishes into the clean (half-emptied) dishwasher, particularly since I'd just asked him (twice) to check the status of the dishwasher before dripping milk all over clean dishes. Most moms get mad about their kids smoking pot or partying, but not me. I'm more discerning than most (insert eye-roll emoji).

Why do I have to be so angry?

Pastor Tim Keller posed a provoking question in a sermon on anger. He said that the next time you get angry, ask yourself, "What is it inside me that makes me so upset?" I love and hate that question all at the same time. I love it because I know finding the answer will help me be less angry, but I hate it because despite asking myself this question many times, I've no idea what's inside me that makes me so angry.

In his book *Tattoos on the Heart*, Father Greg Boyle has a chapter entitled "Slow Work" where he talks about waiting. "Ours is a God who waits. Who are we not to? It takes what it takes for the great turnaround. Wait for it."[11] So that's what I'm continuing to do. Waiting for the great turnaround. Waiting for God to show me why I get so angry, irritated, and annoyed with people.

What happens when I "wait for it"? What happens when, instead of getting frustrated that I'm not changing, I wait? What

---

[11] Boyle, Gregory. *Tattoos on the Heart*, 113. New York: Free Press, 2010.

happens when I trust that God will eventually show me what's inside me that makes me so angry?

I learn.

I've realized that my husband, who is brilliant and accomplished, almost never gets irritated by people who think they're smarter than he is. I've learned that I can be jealous of even my dearest friends. I've learned that even when I'm angry, defensive, or condescending, those closest to me (who I most often lash out at) seem quick to forgive me. I've learned that although God's slow work is always loving, patient, and generous, I don't extend that same grace to others who probably don't like how they act sometimes.

Waiting for my great anger turnaround feels inefficient. I'm a freeway-loving, drive-eight-over-the-speed-limit, fast-lane kind of girl, but God in His love is teaching me that being fast is not necessarily being efficient, and there are no quick fixes, so quit expecting them. When I wait, I'm forced to see beautiful, loving, and awful things in myself that I would otherwise miss. Beautiful, loving, and awful things that I need to see if I'm going to get to the root of my rage and disdain toward others. When I wait, I become more comfortable waiting, and that has been a gift of newfound peace and contentment.

What is it in me that makes me so upset? I'm not sure yet, but I know that my family and loved ones are worth me waiting expectantly and patiently for my big turnaround.

• • • •

To Think About

Do you find yourself often thinking that God is slow? Do you grow irritated and frustrated when you have to pray something more than two or three times? I am learning to try to give thanks when God seems to be taking His time. I learn more, my faith grows, and I love Christ more deeply in the waiting.

This week, when you have to wait or you're tired of praying for the same thing, try and thank God. If you can't, tell Him why. Then tell Him again the next day, and the next, and watch what He teaches you along the wait.

A Death in the Family

"He heals the brokenhearted and binds up their wounds."

Psalm 147:3

Week Forty-One

Early one morning, my friend, who is the executive director of the inner-city transitional living facility whose board I serve on, called to tell me that Amanda, a member at Hope Street, had passed away.

What does it mean to be a "member" at Hope Street? Technically, I suppose, a member is someone who lives, pays rent, attends the weekly community meeting, and signs the Hope Street member agreement. But in the last few years that I've been part of the Hope Street community, I know that a member is actually something else as well.

A member is family.

Family at Hope Street is like any family. Family always has your back no matter how messy, neat, complicated, or simple things are. At my house, family argues, gets annoyed, hugs, yells, dislikes, loves, and everything in between on any given day. It's a mix of good and bad, success and failure, truth and grace, and no matter what, our family loves, cares for, and protects its own.

When I arrived at Hope Street that morning, I saw family at its best. Lisa had made phone calls and helped the paramedics working on Amanda. Robie took care of Amanda's two young daughters. Marilyn showed the girls a YouTube video to find out how they liked their eggs cooked, then made them breakfast. Amaya, age 14, hugged the girls for a very long time, then took them to the playroom to color with them. Rhonda, Kim, Brian,

JJ, Angie, Rachael, Ash, Amy, Dawn, Perry, Hannah, Mr. Charles, Victor, Teesa, Jasmine, Ouita, Terrance, and so many more members, staff, and volunteers—all family—came together and did what family does. They loved, cared for, and protected their own. They cried, hugged, helped, and were present because that's what family does.

Everyone knew Amanda because she cleaned our building and assisted the staff. But she did so much more at Hope Street too. When she vacuumed, swept, and served, Amanda always had a smile. She was always grateful. She never complained, argued, or gossiped. She was quick to listen, was never in a hurry, and was an amazing mama to her 4- and 8-year-old girls. Amanda had a way of bringing out the best in the Hope Street family, in life and even in death.

I cried a lot that week. I cried when I first saw the girls. I cried at community prayer, and I cried writing this post. But whenever the unspeakable happens, I know one thing: God is on His throne. I don't know why He allows days like that, but for whatever reason, I am comforted knowing He wasn't shaken or surprised by it. I find some peace trusting that when I'm mad, confused, and broken, God is in charge and can be trusted beyond my emotions, beyond my capacity to understand, and beyond the pain in and around me. Faith in God doesn't happen overnight or easily, but it's the only thing that gets us through those days. When all I see is hurt, faith in Christ's love, plan, and sovereignty is all I have, thanks be to God.

. . . .

To Think About

Have you ever thought about what God is doing when the bottom drops out from under you? What is His heart for you in your pain, stress, or loss? Maybe you don't think or care about God being on His throne. Maybe you're mad, confused, and frustrated. I have often found that I experience my deepest intimacy with Christ in places of pain, struggle, and honest vulnerability. It is difficult, but a sweet blessing, when the Holy Spirit helps me remember to consider God's heart and position toward me in hard places.

This week, ask yourself what God would say to you in your pain. If the answer doesn't bring you to tears, comfort you, and/or remind you how deeply you are loved, check to see if your response lines up with God's Word.

The Tone of God's Voice

"For as high as the heavens are above the earth, so great is his love for those who fear him; as far as the east is from the west, so far has he removed our transgressions from us."

Psalm 103:11-12

Week Forty-Two

In the discipleship group I'm in, we've been learning about identity. Not the identity we say our identity is grounded in, but the honest and awful reality of the identity we live out of. If my identity was based in being Christ's fully-known, fully-loved daughter, I wouldn't have snapped at my husband last week when he thoughtfully brought me my phone. I unfortunately usually identify myself by my failures. Instead of hearing Chris say, "I found your phone," I heard, "Here's your phone you poor, unorganized, and fragmented mess. Let me help you because, clearly, you need it."

"Thank you, honey. Here's your head back."

I'm becoming painfully aware that I'm good at believing God's Word and truths for others, but not for myself. Ironically, I often remind women I speak to that they need to give themselves the same grace they give others. If your BFF made a mistake, you wouldn't chastise her, call her names, or deem her a complete failure, but that's what we often do to ourselves. I love that advice, believe it is helpful, and want women to put it into practice, but there's one problem.

It doesn't work.

I've tried telling myself that there's no condemnation for those in Christ Jesus (Romans 8:1). I love the verse in Zephaniah about God rejoicing over us with singing, and I want that, but the voices in my head that tell me I'm not enough are louder, more persistent, and much more convincing. What's awesome about my discipleship group though is that it isn't helpful to say or think what we don't believe. We aren't expected to be "further along."

But we also don't stay where we are.

There are many things in the group that we're learning to do, ask, and pray when we struggle, but today, I realized why all that doing, asking, and praying hasn't helped me much. When we get to the root of whatever our struggle is (for me, it's attacking my husband like I'm a grizzly and he's a rabbit when he tries to do nice things for me), we come up with a short sentence, based on Scripture, that God would say to us about our false belief (i.e. false beliefs that we're unorganized, incompetent, or useless). Today, our group leader told one of the women not only to pray about the truth from Scripture that God would say to her about the lie she'd been telling herself, but also to say it tenderly like she was saying it to her daughter. The minute she said that, I realized why giving myself the grace I give others has never worked for me.

I don't love me like God does.

God doesn't want me to just read about or tell myself that He loves me, He wants me to feel, see, and taste His love. He wants me to hear Him say that He loves me with the heart, plea, and passion I not only say, but genuinely believe for my kids. He loves us so much that He wants us to consider the tone of His voice for us, and after today, I believe how we hear Him can profoundly impact the depth of our belief of that love.

．．．．

To Think About

How do you hear God? Is He disappointed with you? When you do well, does He nod to you like it's about time you did something good? Is He curt, abrupt, aloof, and quick to condemn you? How we hear God matters.

Take some time this week to listen to how you hear God. Compare the sound of His voice and His demeanor toward you with what Scripture says about His heart toward you. Do they line up?

This, Again?

"God does not give us overcoming life;
He gives us life as we overcome."

Oswald Chambers

Week Forty-Three

I recently blogged about how I'm trying to figure out what it is in me that makes me react to people so often with anger, sarcasm, and irritability. I also talked about how long it seems to be taking the Lord to help me analyze, understand, and ultimately fix the enigma known as me.

In my discipleship class, we're learning about the Biblical definition of identity. I'm learning that my identity doesn't come from my role as mom, my inability to perform basic math, or my absurdly small forehead. I am not comprised of the things I like or don't like about my personality, appearance, or temperament. My identity is defined by Christ's unconditional grace and love. Christ has made me new, so I am holy, blameless, and free, no matter my forehead size.

The problem with this is that although I love Jesus, call myself a Christian, and believe all of this cerebrally, I don't live like I believe it. When someone recently accused me of doing something wrong when I was trying to help someone else, I was enraged. I was extremely irritated with another individual who was being condescending toward me. After writing a blog post about my hostile tone with my son, I've done the exact same thing to him and my husband multiple times since.

I was explaining this dichotomy to my friend who facilitates my discipleship group. I told her that although I believed everything we were learning about identity, I struggle to live caring only about God's approval. In fact, I think I'm getting more upset, easily offended, and hostile by the minute. I told her that I felt like the more I asked God to show me why I act this way, the more He's taking one of those big circus spotlights and illuminating more brightly what I already know.

I'm a hot mess.

When I told my friend this, she looked me in the eyes and said, "You're exactly where you are supposed to be." She reminded me of the exact thing I had blogged about just last week but had forgotten because I didn't like it: I must wait for the slow work of God. She told me I had to "sit in my weeds" because that's where God meets us.

I didn't get here overnight. I've beaten myself, worried about and tried to manage the opinions of others, and had a hot temper for forty-some-years. Yet somehow, I expect God to help me live fully steeped in my identity in Him in twenty-five seconds.

Although I'm less than happy that I'm now adding "weed dwelling" along with waiting on God to do His work in me, it is here you shall find me.

· · · ·

To Think About

In editing this book and rereading several years of blog posts chronicling my life lessons, I'm realizing that many of the things I struggle with in life and faith seem to be the same things over and over again. Part of me finds that embarrassing to admit, but it's also the reason I wanted to write this book. I don't think my propensity to struggle with the same things repeatedly is unique to me. I believe it is in the places we continue to fail that we are hardest on ourselves and the most frustrated.

Why do I want to share the fact that I seem to wrestle with the same five personality flaws over and over with you? Because that's life. Because that is why Christ came. Because it is in the mundane mistakes we default to that we find and experience God's grace and are drawn more intimately to His love. It is also the place we will begin to find more freedom, joy, and abundant living.

This week, if you wrestle with something you've wrestled before, do not grow weary, fellow traveler! God is conforming us to Christ's likeness (Romans 8:29) day by day.

When Your Friend Gets Robbed

"Christianity means community through Jesus Christ and in Jesus Christ. No Christian community is more or less than this. Whether it is a brief, single encounter or the daily fellowship of years, Christian community is only this. We belong to one another only through and in Jesus Christ."

Dietrich Bonhoeffer

Week Forty-Four

I went to community prayer at Hope Street this week, the transitional living facility I volunteer at in the heart of Milwaukee's inner city. I hadn't planned on going, and I didn't really have time. But earlier in the week, the executive director emailed our board letting us know that the building had been burglarized, and I knew I needed to, as our executive director calls it, *just show up.*

Charles began the prayer time reading a devotional, coincidentally on fear. It began with a quote from Karl A. Menninger which I found profound, "Fears are educated into us, and can, if we wish, be educated out." When he finished reading, Charles said that he had heard the night before that the building had been burglarized, so he had some trouble sleeping.

I choked back tears. Charles has over the past two years become a dear friend and mentor to me. I hated that my friends had their homes and hearts violated by some intruder.

Another member in our group who walks with a cane and is legally blind was shocked to hear about the robbery. "This place is amazing, man! I no longer have to live out of my car. I got a place to wash my clothes. Why in the heck would you want to steal from this place? That pisses me off. Why would anyone steal from this place when they'd literally give you the shirt off their back?"

I choked back more tears. This already vulnerable man

wasn't worrying about himself. He was angry because someone had violated the trust and property of the staff he loved and who he knew clearly loved him.

Charles then asked if and how we forgive whoever it was who broke into Hope Street. The members talked about Christ's forgiveness and shared stories. They decided that despite their anger and fears, since they'd been forgiven, they must and desired to also forgive.

Another member, Angie, fearful about the break-in, came in late and asked about how we overcome fear with faith. Charles reread the devotional, "We can simply open ourselves to the possibility that things can turn out well." I thought about that idea all day and have several times since.

Then Charles closed in prayer, asking God to increase our faith…"just enough for today."

When I went to community prayer at Hope Street, I wanted to show up and help others, but in the end, as it almost always happens at Hope Street, they helped me. The "broken" men, women, and children at Hope Street taught me humility, gratitude, and the beauty of community. They reminded me what to focus on in order to have more peace. They showed me what matters and what doesn't and how hard it is to fail to forgive others when you've been forgiven. They reminded me how much I love them and how sometimes "just showing up" blesses us more than it does anyone else.

· · · ·

 [12] Wright, N.T. *John For Everyone*, 71. Louisville: Westminster John Knox Press, 2004.

To Think About

Is community difficult for you? It is for me. Even though I'm generally an extrovert, community often makes me feel vulnerable and uncomfortable. However, theologian N.T. Wright reminds us that "there is no such thing as a solitary Christian."[12] I have to force myself oftentimes to remain in community, but I'm learning, just like any discipline of the faith, that community isn't about me, but it does bless me.

This week, do not give up meeting in Christian community!

Finally Free

"Jesus answered him, 'I tell you
the truth, today you will be
with me in paradise.'"

Luke 23:43

Week Forty-Five

Several years ago, I met a woman named Jane. She told me when we met that she struggled with alcoholism, but wished she didn't.

This week, I spoke at her funeral.

The week before the funeral, I met Jane's family and found out more about her. She raised three boys as a single mom and loved to garden, cook, and decorate. She let her boys have a food fight on the last day of their vacations up north (aka coolest mom ever). Jane decorated their home to the hilt for every holiday and sent her boys balloons for their birthdays, even, much to their horror, once they started high school. Jane's boys, all grown men now, say that their mom is their hero.

What do you picture when you picture a "good" Christian?

Perhaps you envision someone with well-behaved kids and a wonderful marriage. Maybe you picture Billy Graham or Mother Teresa or someone else who would never swear, gossip, or drink fermented beverages.

I picture Jane.

Jane got Jesus. Jane had her struggles, but in the midst of them, she was humble, caring, and genuine. She wasn't afraid to admit her weaknesses, she smiled during her struggles, and she loved everyone. Jane didn't judge others because she was too busy working on improving Jane.

What about the alcoholism?

What about my road rage I often write about and lament over, but keep doing? What about how I had to apologize to my 14-year-old yet again for the degrading and demeaning way I recently spoke to her? What about when I judge others (daily) or call someone a name in front of my son because they looked at me the wrong way?

Alcoholism, gossip, pride, anger, judgment...

What about all our struggles?

Jane got Christianity like most of us don't. No matter how much prettier or acceptable we think our sins may be compared to others, the Bible is clear: God is holy and perfect and cannot tolerate sin, no matter how inconsequential we may rationalize our sin to be (after all, other people's sins are always uglier and more obvious to us than our own).

That's where Jesus comes in. Jane understood in complete humility who she was in Jesus despite her choices and things she wished looked differently. She understood that Christianity isn't about how we perform or where we fail, it's about loving God and loving others (Matthew 22:36-39). She understood what Phillips Brooks said, "Grace does not depend on what we have done for God but rather what God has done for us. Ask people what they must do to get to heaven, and most reply, 'Be good.' Jesus' stories contradict that answer. All we must do is cry, 'Help!'"

God bless you, Jane. Because of Christ's death, I know we will meet again. I'm grateful for that because I wish I had known you better in this short life. You are missed immensely by the men you raised so well and who you taught to love and accept others, just like you did.

• • • •

To Think About

_____

Is there a group of people, a category of sin, or a behavior you don't think is forgivable? Outside the pregnancy center where I volunteer, a man recently shot a mother, right in front of her 17-year-old son, after the man ran into her car. I struggle with crimes against children. I have prayed to the Lord about this when a child near my hometown watched her parents get murdered, then was abducted from her home and held captive for several months. I could not pray for the perpetrator.

It is tempting to ignore thoughts like this, isn't it? Who wants to think about these things, let alone pray about them? However, processing the hard parts of faith and the Bible are critical to understanding salvation, grace, and the Christian life. We must continually question what we believe about God in order to believe more deeply.

Oswald Chambers once said, "We begin our Christian life by believing what we are told to believe, then we have to go on to so assimilate our beliefs that they work out in a way that redounds to the glory of God. The danger is in multiplying the acceptation of beliefs we do not make our own."

This week, pray honestly about what you believe and what you doubt. It's in those hard prayers that we grow to trust God more!

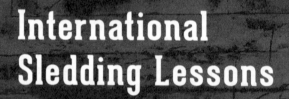

International Sledding Lessons

"Do not conform to the pattern of this world, but be transformed by the renewing of your mind."

Romans 12:2a

Week Forty-Six

My discipleship group will be over soon. No more meetings at seven thirty in the morning. No more feeling Naked and Afraid. This group has been like no other Bible study, discipleship course, or curriculum I've experienced, and I have grown, changed, and been challenged. How?

I've learned to make new tracks.

A few weeks ago, I took our Chinese exchange student sledding. He was excited but nervous since he'd never gone before. After a few successful rides, Zu had a pretty good wipeout, so we headed to the kiddie hill. After Zu climbed up the short embankment, I realized just how foreign sledding was for him. Instead of sledding down one of the many existing paths, Zu went down an untouched part of the "hill." He went down on his stomach, very slowly, gradually amassing a large pile of snow on his neck and chin.

As he went back up the hill, I told him to go down the track he'd just made. This time it was easier and more fun. Eventually, Zu was sailing down his new track, unimpeded and with great joy.

Our discipleship group facilitator commented recently about the science of renewing our minds. She talked about how things we do, think, and say repeatedly form literal tracks in our brains. Those tracks become our default, the part of the "hill" we always go down because it's familiar, easy, and habitual.

Making new tracks, thinking and responding differently, is uncomfortable. It's slow, boring, and takes effort.

However, just like the joy Zu experienced after making his own new tracks, there is much joy in thinking, acting, and speaking differently. There is freedom in listening to what God says rather than riding down my familiar tracks of self-deprecation. I'm finding purpose in learning to hear God's voice in a loving way rather than the voice of shame and anger I used to mistakenly hear Him in. I'm experiencing less regret in making new tracks too. Tracks that help me quit looking back and gravitating to fear, and tracks that help me feel and live out of God's real, tangible, and visible love more often.

When Zu wiped out on the big hill, he lost his glasses. He was looking all over trying to find them, but it's hard to see when you can't see. I quickly slipped down the hill and told Zu to make sure no one took me out while I looked for his glasses. We can't find our glasses or make new tracks alone. We need each other. I was reminded of that often in the past year. People are difficult, like the lady who told me while I was running to help Zu, "You shouldn't wear glasses sledding." Thank you. Super helpful right now (eye-roll emoji). I'm difficult. Life is difficult. But part of being a disciple and being discipled is the reality that people are the point of the cross: me, you, and annoying sled lady.

How do you grow as a disciple?

Go sledding with some friends.

• • • •

To Think About

Where do you want to make new tracks? Where can you begin to memorize and meditate on Scripture to renew your thinking? Are you a glass half-empty person? Look for a verse about gratitude. Perhaps you are good at beating yourself up. Romans 8:1 would be a great verse to memorize.

The caveat to creating new tracks grounded in God's truth is that God's Word must be combined with faith (Hebrews 4:2).

This week, remember to ask the Lord to help you not only memorize verses, but grow in your awareness of His love for you. Making new tracks requires our minds and hearts to believe God's truths more deeply!

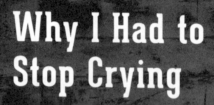

Why I Had to Stop Crying

"Our lives begin to end the day
we become silent about things
that matter."

Martin Luther King Jr.

Week Forty-Seven

A few years ago, after the school shooting in Parkland, Florida, I couldn't stop crying. I cried because the children who were killed were the same age my daughter was at the time, 15. I cried because two sets of parents had empty beds in their homes. I cried because I was so tired of the violence, especially to children, and I cried because I couldn't do anything about it.

Or could I?

As I cried and prayed after this horrific tragedy, I kept thinking about a quote by Mother Teresa:

"...I feel that the greatest destroyer of peace today is abortion, because it is a war against the child – a direct killing of the innocent child – murder by the mother herself. And if we accept that a mother can kill even her own child, how can we tell other people not to kill one another?"

As I lamented another school shooting (the 11th since January 1st), I realized that it wasn't about what I could do to end violence, it's about what I couldn't do:

"Rescue those being led away to death; hold back those staggering toward slaughter. If you say, 'But we knew nothing about this,' does not he who weighs the heart perceive it? Does not he who guards your life know it? Will he not repay each person according to what they have done?" (Proverbs 24:11-12).

I couldn't be okay with doing nothing anymore. I couldn't cry, feel bad, pray, and then forget. I couldn't reconcile some recent statistics I heard: Under Stalin's regime, 40 million people were murdered, and under Hitler, 30 million. Since Roe v. Wade, in the United States alone, 55 million babies have been killed. Regardless of who I vote for or what I think about women's rights and the science of when a fetus is a human, I'm not okay with those numbers, and I couldn't be silent anymore.

So, what did I decide to do? I prayed about it for a long time, and here's what I concluded: the answer is always love. I'm going to love by not judging those who have had abortions (many of my friends have). Love by having empathy instead of criticism toward women with unwanted pregnancies. Love by supporting pregnancy centers and organizations who don't shame, guilt, or pressure women, but who provide support and compassionate options for moms-to-be. Love by praying for women, doctors, and nurses at both abortion and pro-life clinics. I'm going to love by being a small voice for the voiceless. I'm going to love by doing.

"Dear Lord, Please provide peace and comfort to the families involved in the shooting in Parkland, including the family of the shooter, a child himself. Show us what to do about all this, Lord. Help us be hands and feet that aren't cliché, lifeless, and numb. Be our voice. Wake us up and keep us from living a life of apathy, devoid of conviction, and missing countless opportunities to love others. The stakes are too high.

In Jesus' Name, Amen."

• • • •

To Think About

What can you do to help protect victims of abortion? There have been seasons where praying for the unborn, their mothers, abortion-minded doctors, insurance companies, and politicians on both sides of the issue was what I could do. In those busy seasons, I realized that my good intentions sometimes seemed to get lost and forgotten quickly and easily, so I would put reminders in prominent places to help me pray consistently. Recently, in a new season of life where I have had more flexibility with my time and schedule, I am volunteering weekly at a local pregnancy center.

This week, pray and decide, in the season you are in right now, what can you do?

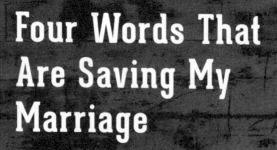

Four Words That Are Saving My Marriage

"A quarrelsome wife is like the dripping of a leaky roof in a rainstorm."

Proverbs 27:15

Week Forty-Eight

Lately, God's been saving my marriage.

Not that my marriage is failing, at-risk, or problematic, but God, in His grace, wants to keep it that way.

Several years ago, I began praying about how I talk to my kids. I realized that I would do things like spend the only half hour I had with them before school yelling, correcting, and criticizing them. Of course, I'd also give them a hug and send them out the door telling them that I loved them (in case that wasn't obvious amidst all the nagging and rage). After I began praying about this, I got ideas like not disciplining them in the morning. I would instead write down anything I felt needed their attention, so that after school, when we had more time, I could address with them their failures as human beings. Generally, however, I would toss the list by noon. Once my sanity returned and I wasn't rushing around, the shoes they left out, glass they forgot to wash, and other minor offenses in the grand scheme of things didn't seem so colossal.

Unfortunately, over the years, I've not been as prayerful about how I address my husband. I've not been as remorseful over my verbal tyranny, critical spirit, and irrational responses to him. I have to some degree, but not to the extent I had with our children.

Until our children left.

Now that two of our kids are at college and the third one

drives, we are alone. A lot. We are home together. A lot. I have more time to focus on Chris and to nag, correct, and criticize him too.

When I noticed that I was hyper-focusing on my husband's every move and misstep, I began praying about it, and God answered me with four words. Almost every time I'm about to correct Chris for something petty, cleanliness-related, or otherwise not worth mentioning (that I can't keep myself from mentioning), I hear the four words. I hear them right when I need them and just before I verbally vomit things that make my husband feel incompetent, unappreciated, and mothered. The four words are simple and direct:

"Leave the man alone."

"Leave the man alone" has helped me avoid correcting what doesn't matter. It's helped me pause long enough to remember that my husband has a successful career where he manages people, finances, deadlines, and more. All without my help. "Leave the man alone" reminds me that my husband is a man, and if my 19-year-old son resents my smothering, imagine how my 50-something-year-old husband feels about it.

How has God been saving my marriage? By helping me put my husband before the condition of my house. By showing me how easily pride can seep into my heart. By speaking the truth in love to me in a way I can receive, process, and obey it best.

Simply and directly.

• • • •

To Think About

If you're married, are you an expert at correcting your spouse? Has your nagging helped "train" him? I remember once hearing a Christian speaker who begged her husband for over fifty years to use a plate for his toast. One day, he looked at his adoring wife and said, "I think we both know I'm never going to use a plate for my toast." She laughed but lamented that story. Her husband passed away shortly after that. She wished she wouldn't have majored on the minors in their marriage.

This week, let's continue to pray that God would bless our marriages and help open our eyes to places where we can be an encouragement and blessing to our husbands.

"**Help**"

"For when I am weak,
then I am strong."

2 Corinthians 12:10b

Week Forty-Nine

The holidays were hard this year. Perhaps I had PTSD after my dad's heart attack. Maybe it was all my friends who had lost a parent or loved one recently. Maybe it was my daughter Hannah amassing things for her apartment (a collection rivaling inventory at HomeGoods) or my son Casey's college tour reminding me of the season of lasts we were in. I'm not sure why, but every Christmas song, commercial, and decoration was depressing, and I began to understand why some people struggle in December.

I knew I had no reason to be down. My dad not only survived his major heart attack earlier this year, but he was doing quite well. Although many friends were grieving first Christmases without loved ones, by God's grace I wasn't. As sad as I was to see my twenty-year career as a stay-at-home mom come to an end, no one wants their kids living in their basement until they're 40 (for our sake and theirs). Realizing this should've made me snap out of my funk. Being aware of all I had to be thankful for should've given me joy.

But it didn't.

On my dad's worst day in the ICU, I remember driving home bawling and praying out loud, "God, please help him..." over and over again. It was all I could pray because I was exhausted, empty, and helpless. There wasn't anything the doctors or I could do to help my dad feel or get better. I got home around ten thirty that night and asked anyone who was awake and on social media to pray for my dad, and immediately, they did.

When I went to see my dad that next morning, I asked him how he slept. He hadn't slept more than a few hours at a time since arriving in the ICU four days earlier. He said, "I closed my eyes around ten thirty and slept for about seven hours." Although I know prayer doesn't usually work that way, I've been finding that when I come to the end of myself and can't control the situation, pain, or funk I'm in, my prayers are simple, passionate, and more effective.

How did I break the Christmas blues I shouldn't have had, but did? I asked. I asked God to take them away because I couldn't make them go away. How could I explain my sadness lifting after simply repeating those few, desperate words? The same way I'd explain my dad going from extreme pain to sleeping like a baby.

I can't.

I want empirical evidence or some articulate explanation, but that's how humans work. The Holy Spirit doesn't roll that way. As much as I don't always like how God and the Holy Spirit work, I'm finally beginning to understand more fully what the Bible means when it talks about Christ's strength being made perfect in weaknesses (2 Corinthians 12:8-10). No one wants to be or admit that they're weak, but unfortunately, I seem to keep finding myself unable to help myself. The irony is, as I stand helpless to do anything but hope and watch, I'm finding it's a pretty amazing view.

· · · ·

To Think About

When was the last time you simply prayed, "Help"? What situation, relationship, or struggle seems too big, difficult, or overwhelming? Try merely asking God for help for a few hours, days, and weeks. Romans 8:26 says, "...the Spirit helps us in our weakness. We do not know what we ought to pray for, but the Spirit himself intercedes for us through wordless groans."

This week, ask for help, then watch, wait, and listen. You'll probably need to keep asking, watching, waiting, and listening, but Psalm 34:15 says that God is attentive to the cries of the righteous. In Christ, the Bible says we have been made righteous (1 Corinthians 1:30, 2 Corinthians 5:21), so don't give up crying out for help, dear sister.

The [New] Voices in My Head

"Now to him who is able to do
immeasurably more than all we
can ask or imagine, according to
his power that is at work within us."

Ephesians 3:20

Week Fifty

One of the things I've been learning in my discipleship group is how to replace the voices in my head with God's. There are a few caveats associated with this, however. One is that I have to know God's voice (the Bible), and the second is that I need to identify the emotions, voices, and subconscious thoughts that need replacing.

One prevalent "voice" that I listen to has been around a long time. Like most voices in my heart and head, the need to control is subtle but constant. Since I've gotten better at not verbally manipulating others, I thought I wasn't what my friend calls "over-functioning." However, I'm learning that overthinking, planning, and constantly worrying are other means of over-functioning and are just as unhealthy, damaging, and disabling to myself and others.

What's wrong with mentally over-functioning? What's dysfunctional about playing and replaying in my mind the ways I can "help" my kids with their financial and life decisions and their relationships? What's the harm in lying awake pondering if my husband disciplined one of our kids "correctly"? Although we are supposed to coach our young adult children, obsessing over their life choices and trying to manipulate outcomes on their behalf actually disempowers them.

It's not good for me either. Last month, I chewed through an appliance I wear because I grind my teeth incessantly. I've had difficulty falling and staying asleep this week. I've cried more in the past seven days about parenting and marital issues than I have in the past six months. Why?

I'm over-functioning.

So now what? How do I begin replacing the voice that tells me I need to try to fix everything and protect everyone with God's voice? How do I begin loosening my grip of control?

Ralph Waldo Emerson said, "What lies behind us and what lies before us are tiny matters compared to what lies within us." What does the Bible say lies inside those of us who know and love Jesus Christ? "Now to him who is able to do immeasurably more than all we can ask or imagine, according to his power that is at work in us" (Ephesians 3:20).

What lies within us is power if we pray instead of plan. What lies within us is unimaginable, not the unthinkable. Starting today, I'm replacing worry and over-functioning with Ephesians 3:20. I'm asking God to help me trust His ability to solve more than mine. Starting today, instead of worrying about what happened yesterday or might happen tomorrow, I'm going to try and believe this verse. Then I'm going to watch what God does...

Starting today.

• • • •

To Think About

Where, when, and with whom are you over-functioning? Maybe you're like me and don't think you are.

This week, pray and ask God to show you if you are mentally, verbally, or emotionally trying to control people, relationships, or situations. Then ask for help trusting Him instead. Usually, we over-function with the people who mean the most to us. God understands that, which is why He wants to help free us from burdens we were never meant to carry.

Fear of Snow

"The growth of trees and plants takes place so slowly that it is not easily seen. Daily we notice little change. But, in course of time, we see that a great change has taken place. So it is with grace. Sanctification is a progressive, lifelong work (Proverbs 4:18). It is an amazing work of God's grace and it is a work to be prayed for (Romans 8:27)."

John Owen

Week Fifty-One

Does God "work"?

I have battled anxiety and panic attacks since I was five years old, and although praying, memorizing Scripture, and gaining a deeper understanding of who God is has liberated me from many anxiety issues and the heavy weight that comes from being in slavery to fear, I still battle it more than I'd like, and frankly, I'm tired of it.

I understand that God isn't a genie and His ways aren't our ways. I understand that we live in a fallen world (thanks again, Eve) and that everything will be made new someday. But struggling with anxiety once again has me wondering if God works. Does He change anything long-term? Does He matter in the hard places and the recurring places we should have moved on from by now?

My latest fear is weather-induced. Snow, to be exact. My son got his learner's permit in November, and my 17-year-old is driving kids daily for her job as a nanny. When the snow started to fall, I became incredibly anxious about my kids being behind the wheel. Not your everyday, run-of-the-mill, normal, motherly-type worrying, but the kind of worrying that keeps me up at night, induces eye twitches, and keeps me constantly preoccupied with what-ifs.

As it typically happens when I'm in a season of doubt, frustration, or confusion about God, I'm still reading my Bible, journaling, and praying. I asked the Lord to show me what it looked like to "seek peace and pursue it." Another day, I journaled about what it meant to "...not fear what they fear" (Isaiah 8:12b), but the more I prayed and read my Bible, the more frustrated I grew that fear seemed once again to be winning the battle for my time, attention, and mental energy. Then, after reading about a local teengage driver fighting for her life after being in a horrific car accident, I gave up. I asked God in frustrated exhaustion to supernaturally remove my anxieties because nothing I was studying, praying about, or looking to seemed to be working.

To me, God "working" would mean the total elimination of fear in my life. It would mean no more victories over anxiety a thousand times just to find something new to worry about tomorrow. But I'm realizing that God "working" means exactly what He has been doing for the last twenty years of my ongoing battle with anxiety, including, but not limited to, my fear of snow.

It is through prayer, confronting my doubts and frustrations with God, and reading His Word that I slowly, repeatedly, and more deeply discover more of who God is. In that process of discovery, I learn to trust Him more, resist the urge to control that which isn't in my control (everything), and rediscover the hope I have in Him, over and over and over again. God is gradually but consistently taking away my fear of snow, and He will help me work through the next anxiety as well.

Oswald Chambers said, "It is the process, not the end, which is glorifying to God." God "works" by constantly being at work in me. The process isn't pretty, instantaneous, or once-and-done, but His work creates lasting incremental change and, best of all, delivers hope when we need it most.

· · · ·

To Think About

Would you trust, love, or have a "need" to know God better, or at all, if everything you struggle with was suddenly fixed or removed? God did not intend for us to live in fear, but I'm trying to find gratitude when I am in a place of dependency on Him. It is in the hard places that I am afforded the opportunity to know His love and care for me more deeply, intimately, and passionately.

This week, thank God that you need Him and that in that place of dependency, you are brought to places of greater faith and intimacy with Him.

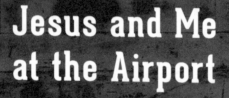

Jesus and Me at the Airport

"I love those who love me; And those who diligently seek me will find me."

Proverbs 8:17 (NASB)

Week Fifty-Two

Earlier this year, I attended an upsetting funeral. Upsetting because the pastor ended his sermon, in the most genuine, heartfelt, and believable way, talking about how awesome it will be at the end of our lives to run into the arms of Jesus. He said that he couldn't imagine a sweeter, more perfect place than in Christ's embrace. Why would that be upsetting?

Because I could.

I love Jesus, but I love earth too. I love my kids, husband, friends, feather pillow, and coffee. I say that I love Jesus more than anything, and I do love Him, but I love what's familiar, safe, and known more. I can't touch Jesus or look Him in the eyes. My relationship with Christ isn't the same as it is with the humans I interact with daily.

So, after the funeral, I began asking Him for help.

I told God that I wanted Him to be the most important thing in my life, but I didn't know what that looked like or how to get there. I told Him that, for some reason, it was scary to think about loving Him more than I did my husband or kids. For many weeks in many different ways, I asked God to help me love Him...most.

And one day, He responded.

One morning, while praying on a walk, my mind wandered. I thought about when my son flew alone for the first time last spring. I remembered how excited I was waiting at the airport for Casey. We hadn't been apart long, but I missed him and couldn't wait to see him. I scanned the terminal while hundreds of people walked past, blocking my line of vision. I waited with heightened anticipation for what seemed like forever, until I eventually spotted my son. When I finally saw his smiling face, my heart leapt.

I don't remember what made me think of the airport scene while I was praying, but as I kept walking on that beautiful, sunny morning, I distinctly remember what happened next.

God gave me a picture.

I looked up at the clouds and suddenly thought about Jesus coming down from heaven. He was looking for something. He was scanning all around, his eyes darting back and forth while He got closer and closer. Then His eyes met mine, and He stopped and smiled...

And His heart leapt.

Tears filled my eyes as I finished my walk. I didn't instantly long to be with God, but in the sweetness of that moment, He stirred my affections for Him. He made His view of me personal. He reminded me that He didn't just die for me—He delights in me.

And in that moment, I realized that I could never quit asking God for more, to love and know Him more and to know His love more. We cannot exhaust God's love or know Him completely. And although I'm not holding a candlelight vigil for my impending death, God's moved me closer to trusting the sweetness of His embrace.

. . . .

To Think About

What honest reservations do you have about God, heaven, the Bible, and faith? Where do you want to believe something about Jesus, but you really don't? Are you willing to tell God about those doubts this week? Sometimes I think we are afraid to tell the Lord what we don't really believe about Him, but of course, He already knows. So why tell Him? To open your heart, mind, and imagination for Him to speak love into more freely and intimately.

About
the Author

Laura Sandretti is a wife, mom, and Christian author and speaker. She formerly worked as a high school special education teacher and director of women's ministries, but more recently, Laura volunteers and writes curriculum for Care Net, a pregnancy center located in the heart of Milwaukee. She also serves as the board chair for Hope Street Ministry, a Christian transitional living facility in the inner city. Laura recently earned a master's degree in theological studies from Trinity Evangelical Divinity School.

Laura has been married for twenty-seven years to her husband Chris, and they have two kids in college and one in high school. As their nest empties, Laura and Chris enjoy bicycling and walking in the summer, and during the nine winter months in Wisconsin, they enjoy cross-country skiing. Laura also enjoys photography, hot coffee, and cool cars.

Imperfectly Perfect is Laura's second book. Her first book, *Walking By the Homeless*, has raised thousands of dollars for Hope Street Ministry and has reminded readers that God doesn't call everyone to do something big in Jesus' name, but He does call us all to do something. To find out more about Laura or *Walking By the Homeless*, visit www.everydaysinner.com.

CPSIA information can be obtained
at www.ICGtesting.com
Printed in the USA
JSHW011043061219
2830JS00003B/9